MIKE HEBERT
THE FIRE STILL BURNS

Mike Hebert with Dave Johnson

SAGAMORE PUBLISHING
Champaign, IL

©1993 Mike Hebert
All rights reserved.

Production supervision and interior design: Michelle R. Dressen
Dustjacket and photo insert design: Michelle R. Dressen
Editor: Dan Heaton
Proofreader: Phyllis L. Bannon

Library of Congress Catalog Card Number: 93-84958
ISBN: 0-915611-77-5

Printed in the United States.

For
CAPTAIN ROBERT R. HEBERT,
a belated thank you for getting me started
in the right direction.

Acknowledgments vi
Prologue ix

Chapter 1   Unanswered Questions 1
Chapter 2   Net Gain 13
Chapter 3   Science Alfresco 25
Chapter 4   Teaching, Learning 33
Chapter 5   The Whole World is Watching 41
Chapter 6   Iron City Sojourn 53
Chapter 7   Go West 67
Chapter 8   Talking Trash 81
Chapter 9   From Less Than Zero 93
Chapter 10   Record Breakers 105
Chapter 11   Victory Cigars 119
Chapter 12   Orbiting in Ohio 133
Chapter 13   Rock Bottom 145
Chapter 14   Back Where We Belong 157
Chapter 15   Cardinal Rules 171
Chapter 16   Epilogue 183

ACKNOWLEDGMENTS

How does one glance back over almost 50 years of one's life and select a handful of names to include in an acknowledgment? It's an impossible assignment. But I'll take a shot at it.

I could not have survived my early years without the support of my family. My father, to whom this book is dedicated, was a wonderful man and provided the greatest role model imaginable. Lola (Burke) Hebert, my mother, has always believed in me. There is no greater gift a parent can give to a child. My brother, Rich, has taught me volumes about loyalty and commitment. And I always feel warm when I call back the memory of my late sister, Pam, who I lost to a fatal auto accident in 1968. My family was very close, and those of us who survive remain so today.

Sherry Hebert, my wife, and our two daughters, Becky and Hillary, have been rock solid in their support of me as I careen from highs to lows and back again. The life of a coach is a roller coaster ride without a seat belt. And I've been lucky to have three loved ones watching out for me.

A special thank you goes to Dr. Karol Kahrs, Associate Athletic Director at Illinois, for clearing the way so that our volleyball program could continue to grow. Her belief in me and the sport of volleyball has meant a great deal to me over the past ten years.

My coaching style has been impacted by so many during my 33 years in the sport. Here are some individuals who come to mind. I like Doug Beal's confidence in doing things *his* way and demanding that everyone buy into his scheme. I like Dave Shoji's competitiveness and keen eye for game adjustments. I like to watch Sue Woodstra and Debbie Brown work with players. They are both winners. I respect Shelton Collier's uncanny eye for what it takes to win matches. I will always remember Chuck Erbe for his unswerving commitment to his own technical style of training. I am impressed by Terry Pettit, Don Shaw, and Mick Haley for their ability to produce consistently good teams over many years. I appreciate the professional manner in which Andy Banachowski and John Dunning have handled themselves and their programs. I love to watch Russ Rose's teams play. They work so hard on the court and Russ always gets the most out of his players. To the hundreds I've left off this brief list, thank you, too.

I also want to mention my assistant coaches here at Illinois. Even though I'm often listed as his mentor, I've learned more about coaching from Don Hardin than he ever learned from me. I've grown considerably watching Jay Potter insist on sticking to the fundamentals as we attempt to prepare our team for competition. And I've been blessed with presence of a special young talent, Disa Johnson, who I began recruiting in 1982, coached for four years at Illinois, and now enjoy as a member of my coaching staff. These people have been as responsible for our program's success as I've been.

Another group of people come to mind, the media folks in Champaign-Urbana who have covered our sport in an unprecedented fashion. Joe Millas, Fred Kroner, and David Woods of the Champaign-Urbana *News-Gazette* have gone beyond the call of duty in reporting Illinois Volleyball. Jim Turpin, station manager, and Jack Whitman (former sales manager) of WDWS radio made an early commitment to broadcasting our matches. Their station, along with Mike Kelly and his current successor, Dave Loane, have been pioneers in the world of volleyball broadcasting. Dave Dickey of WILL radio, Dan Swaney and Scott Andriesen of WICD-TV, Chris Widlic and John Mayo of WCIA-TV — all of these people have made my time with the local media corps fun, entertaining, and professional.

The University of Illinois Sports Information Office deserves credit for taking us seriously and working long hours to popularize our success. In the beginning, Tom Boeh, and more recently, Dave Johnson have taken a personal interest in figuring out new and creative ways to promote Illinois Volleyball.

And finally, I want to say thank you to the people at Sagamore Publishing for believing that a book about a volleyball coach might work. Joe Bannon and his sons, Joe Jr. and Peter, have been supportive from day one. Dave Johnson's early research and writing, combined with Dan Heaton's marvelous editing and re-writing have breathed life into what might have been a series of unrelated episodes had I been left to my own devices as an author. And thanks to my good friend, Jim Fink, without whose early guidance and advice this project may never have gotten off the ground.

PROLOGUE

"What? Huh?" Finally I just shook my head and shrugged my shoulders. One of my assistant coaches, Disa Johnson, was trying to tell me something, but if it was important, she was going to have to write it down or use sign language. There was no way she was going to make herself heard tonight.

Stanford, ranked No. 2 in the nation, vs. No. 6 Illinois in the NCAA Mideast Regional volleyball final, playing for a spot in the Final Four. Huff Hall was jammed with almost 4,500 fans, making enough noise for 45,000. There was a flash late in Game 1, when we won a rally and looked like we might come back to take the game, when the crowd noise was as intense as in any gym I've ever been in. More than one person who was there that night has told me the same.

Some coaches and athletes claim they never notice the crowd. I've never bought that. I can't imagine anyone being able to block it out completely, and I'm not sure why anyone would want to. When Disa and Jay Potter, my other assistant, were sitting on the bench during the Illinois-Stanford match, our voices completely drowned out by the waves of sound, there was still one thing we could communicate, just by exchanging glances: "Wow, this is special." If you're an athlete, if you're a coach, if you're a fan, this is what you live for, this is what makes it more than a game: to be involved in a contest that has so much riding on it, and to have the support of your home crowd cascading down on you.

Of course, no matter how supportive that wave of noise is, you can't just ride away on it, particularly if you're the coach.

I have to be in control. My job involves constantly monitoring what's happening on the court. I have to guard against too much emotion, to make sure my decisions are based on rational analysis. I have to follow our game plan, not my heart.

Once the match starts, I become so preoccupied with the action, that the crowd noise recedes for the most part into my subconscious. But I'll be flowing along with the match when my ear or my eye will pick up something that takes me away for just a fraction of a second. When I hear our crowd, when that supportive noise breaks through my focus on the match, I'm proud to be involved with this program and those fans. To realize that all those people have taken time out of their lives to come and cheer for my team — what a thrill.

And then I have to shake it off and channel all my focus back onto what's happening on the court. It's my job. I'm the coach.

Unanswered Questions

There's a T-shirt I see around campus from time to time, "Question authority." That's a pretty good philosophy, I think, one I've followed most of my life. So how did I happen to become an authority figure — a coach — myself? Maybe a lot of it has to do with the way my original authority figure, my dad, was taken away from me.

My father was a captain in the Air Force, a bomber pilot. He had grown up in Houston and, like so many of his generation, he joined the military right out of high school. He met my mother during World War II, when he was stationed in California and she was working as an aircraft instrument mechanic. She was a native Californian — a rare breed — and a real-life "Rosie the Riveter."

When Captain Robert R. Hebert landed his B-24 at the end of World War II and came home to Long Beach, he was ready to settle into civilian life with his wife, Lola, and a new member of the family, little Mike, born on January 7, 1944. But when the Korean conflict flared up, he was called up with the Air Force Reserves to fly combat missions. His B-29 departed Kadena Air Force Base in Okinawa on January 30, 1952; it was his last scheduled mission before being sent home. The crew sent a radio message at the 100-mile mark that all was OK. As far as we know, that was the last anyone ever heard from the plane or its crew.

We've never had an acceptable explanation of what happened that night. For years, my mother wrote letters, called politicians, chased every lead, no matter how unpromising. We've requested files from the government, but we've always had the sense they're not telling us everything they know. Was it a secret mission? Had he been captured? Was there a chance he'd survived a crash? Had there even *been* a crash? It's been 40 years and we have never gotten an explanation for what happened to that B-29.

During and after the Vietnam War, I always felt a bond with the families of the MIAs. Missing In Action — such an unemotional, military phrase. For the next of kin, though, there's nothing unemotional about it. Just the reverse; you have too many emotions, but you can't make any sense of them. You feel like mourning, but that would mean giving up. You hold out against despair, but you're afraid to hope. You're in emotional limbo. It would have been easier if there had been a body, or some wreckage of the aircraft. Some tangible evidence of his death would have let us go through a normal grieving process and give the experience some sort of emotional closure. But instead, our lives remained on hold.

I never could come to grips with losing my father under such mysterious circumstances and then having the military treat our loss with such insensitivity. It just doesn't make sense that someone should just slap a telegram in your face at 1 a.m. without showing a little compassion. Losing a parent when you're 8 years old is hell. But losing a parent, and not *knowing* for certain whether you've lost him for good, always wondering, trying not to hope too much, but always wondering: Will Dad come back? Will things be like they're supposed to be again? Will we be a family? And wondering, too, why won't the government, the people we're supposed to trust to preserve the Land of the Free, the Home of the Brave, why won't they tell us all they know about our dad, a man who probably died defending that land? Does that make you question authority just a little bit?

"Our dad," because by now I was the oldest of three kids — Pam was born in 1947 and Richard in 1950 — and so with my father's death I was prematurely *becoming* an authority figure of sorts, the "man of the house." I must have heard that a thousand times from well-meaning relatives and acquaintances: "Now that your father's gone, you have to be the man of the house." I didn't want to be the man of the house. I was a kid, 8 years old; I just wanted my dad.

That contradiction — emotional insecurity on the one hand, an obligation to be emotionally "in charge" on the other —

was the first in a series of defining moments for me. A lot of what I'm about today was born during that episode. I began to develop a strong competitive urge, a will to succeed, but at the same time I was desperately trying to cope with unresolved fears and insecurities. And I acquired a strong sense of justice, and a keen empathy for those who aren't being treated fairly.

I don't want to make it sound like I was some orphan out of a Dickens novel, though. I carved out my own style at a pretty young age, it's true. But I was a California boy, head to toe, and a Baby Boomer all the way. My generation was raised in a period of unblemished optimism. We grew up in the Eisenhower years and entered college with President Kennedy in the White House. The economy was on solid ground and America was the leader of the Free World. There was a tremendous feeling of accomplishment among Americans — we'd pulled out of the depression, won World War II, and we were straightening out the world. For my generation, it was a trouble-free time, people swallowing goldfish, cramming into phone booths, doing the hula-hoop. And in California, that carefree attitude, that optimism and self-satisfaction took its most flamboyant form.

It's become popular to see the Eisenhower era as a time when America just closed its eyes to everything that was wrong, and there's no question that we were ignorant of a lot of the social problems that were just starting to percolate below the surface and would erupt in the late '60s. But the essential optimism in America during that era is one of the biggest positives I took from my childhood. The glass is always half-full for me, and I still feel like any problem can be solved. I'm not sure I'd feel the same way if I'd been born in a different time.

I know I wouldn't have developed that kind of positive outlook without the example provided by my mother. She was incredible, a young woman holding her family together without a husband, and without much support from anyone else. Since my father had never been declared killed in action, we only qualified for a small pension from the government. And my father's family in Texas, who were Catholic, more or less disowned us when Mom wouldn't convert. We were on our own. She earned some money with part-time work, but we always had to count our pennies. Still, she kept our little family together, and she did a remarkable job of it.

That break with Dad's family was part of a pattern that

soured me early on the Catholic Church and on organized religion in general. I had started in a Catholic grade school when my father was still home, and after he was gone, my mother continued to send the three of us to Catholic schools out of respect for him.

Finally, though, it just became too much for us to take. I remember the nuns trying to talk me into moving out of my house and into the convent because my mother wasn't Catholic. The priest came to the house another time, and I heard him tell my mother she'd go to hell if she didn't send us to Catholic school. I'll never forget the phrase he used: "You have a warped mind," he told her, because she didn't think it was necessary to convert. So many of the teachers and administrators at those schools were just closed-minded people, completely insensitive to the needs of a young woman with three kids whose husband's an MIA. Is that Christian behavior? My mother didn't need some hellfire and damnation sermon; she needed a little help and support. But she never got it from the Catholic Church.

In spite of everything, we did our best to be just your average American family. No matter how tight money was, Mom made sure we got to go out to the movies sometimes. Our home was standard Southern California: a stucco ranch-style tract house in a middle-class neighborhood. Behind our house was a little mountain where the neighborhood kids used to build forts, defend our "army" against "invaders."

I had a fairly typical childhood — typical for Southern California, anyway. The freeways were already crowded with commuters into Los Angeles, but there was still lots of open land and open space then. The water was our constant companion. I never swam competitively, but the gang would head to the pool or the ocean every day. I grew up swimming, body-surfing, jumping off diving boards, everything involved with water sports.

Like most little boys, I did some pretty dumb stuff. I remember my cousin Larry Sanders from Riverside and I built a go-cart with a lawn mower engine. Naturally, it caught on fire. Later, we tried to build a surfboard out of two-by-fours and some plywood. As a surfboard, it made a pretty good anchor.

In high school, my friend Dick Neville and I bought a boat kit and spent weeks and weeks putting it together. We built it, painted it, put an outboard motor on it. Finally the big day arrived for the launch, and we hauled it down to the lake and put it in the water. It promptly went nose up. We never could get it to float. I was involved in lots of other equally successful mechanical adventures.

I was interested in sports early on, but I was hardly an immediate success in that arena, either. My first venture, when I was 8 or 9, was baseball. Not Little League, though — Farm League, where they put the kids who aren't good enough for Little League. I remember showing up at the tryout area, and there was the diamond where dads were hitting grounders to their kids. The "in" group had the diamond; that's where all the action was. Me, I got sent out to the far end of the park with some dad who must have been the low man on the Little-League-dads totem pole. There were a dozen of us or so out there shagging fly balls, and this poor Farm League dad had to hit fungos to us for what seemed like forever. Finally it dawned on me that these were the kids who were going to get cut. That's right: my first athletic memory is getting cut from the lowest possible level of organized baseball.

Next I tried football, the equivalent of Pop Warner League. I never was very big for my age, so I quickly became one of the practice players, the guys they tell to run really fast and bang into someone. They tried to call it "blocking" and "tackling," but for me, football was just body sacrifice.

My biggest sports nightmare, though, came back on the baseball diamond a few years later, when I was on a Pony League farm team. I was playing second base one day, and the bases were loaded. The batter hit a slow roller that I should have charged, but I froze. By the time the ball got out to me, it seemed like two or three runs must have scored, and I picked up the ball to wing it home. But the catcher was screaming, "No, no! First base, first base!" So I turned and gunned it so far over the first baseman's head that it hit a car in the parking lot. So much for baseball, at least as a participant.

I got more enjoyment out of being a baseball fan at that stage. I remember cutting out box scores from the newspaper and posting them in a notebook. I knew all the batting averages and could name the players on all the teams in the major leagues.

My loyalties shifted pretty regularly. I started out as a Pirates fan, but then I started rooting for the Yankees—Moose Skowron at first base, Billy Martin at second, Tony Kubek at short, Yogi Berra behind the plate, Whitey Ford on the mound. In the outfield, Hank Bauer, Mickey Mantle, Roger Maris. I remember their great utility infielder Gil McDougald hitting the line drive that shattered Herb Score's eye socket and ruined his career.

I hated the Dodgers for a long time after they beat the Yankees in the 1955 World Series. I really bore a grudge against Johnny Podres, who shut the Yankees out in Game 7. When the Dodgers moved to Los Angeles in 1958, I took it personally: the team that had beaten the Yankees was moving to California just to make me suffer. I must have been the only person in Southern California who didn't welcome the Dodgers.

I never learned to like the team, but a few Dodgers — Gil Hodges, Johnny Roseboro, Maury Wills — eventually joined all my Yankee heroes and Bill Mazeroski and Dick Groat of the Pirates in my personal Hall of Fame. I particularly liked Wills because he had played in an exhibition game in San Bernardino as a minor leaguer before most people had ever heard of him, and I thought he was pretty good then. Naturally, when he broke Ty Cobb's record by stealing 104 bases in 1962, I was proud of my keen eye for talent.

But probably my favorite ballplayer of the time was a minor leaguer, Steve Bilko of the Los Angeles Angels. Now, Bilko played a couple of seasons for the expansion Los Angeles Angels in the American League in the early '60s, but I'm talking about the Angels of the Pacific Coast League. Bilko was a first baseman, and he looked like Babe Ruth. Against minor league pitching, he hit like Ruth, too. Apparently he could never hit a major league curveball, but he hit 55 home runs for the Angels in 1956 and 56 in '57. Steve Bilko — great name, great look, and a great hero to a Southern California kid.

Another Angels player in the early '50s was Chuck Connors, who eventually gave up on baseball and became an actor, TV's "Rifleman." His big rival was the dreaded Hollywood Stars outfielder Carlos Bernier. It seemed like the Angels and Stars played one another all the time, and the games would always be on KTLA, Channel 5, with Dick Lane. You'd see Dick on TV constantly, banging on the fender of a used car in a commercial, announcing baseball, wrestling, roller derby, you name it. It seemed like he'd been doing it for 50 years. He was a California legend.

I remember watching early NBA games, too, which for some reason were televised in California, teams like the Syracuse Nationals, the Minneapolis Lakers and the Fort Wayne Pistons. And football — one time when my dad was still around he took me to the Los Angeles Rams' preseason camp at San Bernardino Valley College. I don't know if it was picture day or autograph day or what — maybe teams just weren't as paranoid about security then — but we walked around the field and met some of the players. I remember seeing Andy Robustelli.

Finally, in junior high school, I began to have a hint of success as a competitor. I made the track team as a long jumper, or rather, as we called it then, a broad jumper. I could always jump pretty well, and I competed in the standing broad jump, the running broad jump, and the triple jump — the hop, skip and jump, it was called then.

Having some success in sports gave a boost to my confidence and my social skills, and believe me, they needed boosting. I played the clarinet in the junior high band, too, having taken lessons as a kid. That wasn't really my first love musically, though. Somewhere along the line, I had developed a taste for rhythm and blues. I remember going to hear a soul group called The Jewels, whose song "Work With Me, Annie" had been banned by all the local radio stations. I enjoyed Dixieland jazz, too, but I didn't really take to rock 'n'roll. To me, Elvis didn't come close to what the black groups were doing. Today, I keep a 90-minute tape of James Brown in the car, and just like when I was a kid, no one else wants to hear my music.

I played in the band in my first year of high school, as well, but I just couldn't overcome my shyness. Part of the cause was the complex of emotions from losing my father, but my years in the Catholic school also contributed to my social backwardness. It was such a protected environment at St. Bernardine's from first through eighth grade that, even after a year at Arrowview Junior High, I was unprepared for the real world when I arrived at San Bernardino High School.

That was a real culture shock, a really difficult adjustment. At the same time, it was something I really needed to experience. In public grade schools, you go to school with the same people you hang out with after school and during the summer. But in Catholic schools, there's nothing like a "school district" — we lived all over the city and got to school on our own.

I don't think any of the other kids in my neighborhood went to St. Bernardine's. It's tough on a kid when you're different. I wish to this day I hadn't had to go to a school outside of my neighborhood. I think it's important to hang out with people who live around you, to have that sense of community and be accepted by your peers.

After an unpromising beginning, I finally was able to gain some of that acceptance through sports. As a tenth grader, I went out for tennis and earned my first varsity letter. The following year, I went out for basketball and made the "B" team, playing guard and forward. I started to develop some skills in basketball, and that helped me develop some confidence as well. I made the varsity as a senior and became the starting point guard. By the end of the season, I was good enough to make third-team all-conference. That's not much, but it was a big boost for me.

I started to develop some confidence off the court, as well, getting involved in other extracurricular activities. I was finally starting to come out of my shell and participate in things. I became sports editor of the school newspaper and was elected vice president of the senior class.

Another important lesson started when I was growing up in San Bernardino and continued at the public high school: not everybody looked like me. St. Bernardine's hadn't been all-white, but it had been pretty close. I remember in seventh and eighth grade, our football team had no practice field so we would bus down to a field in the middle of the project housing. It was a tough neighborhood and here we were, seventh and eighth graders, almost all of us white, middle-class, trying to play football. We could feel the tension, we sensed that the blacks living in the projects didn't really want us using their field, but all we learned from it was that we could feel like outsiders.

Then we got to San Bernardino High School, where there were roughly 3,800 kids, pretty evenly split among Hispanics, blacks, and whites. I quickly grew to appreciate the multicultural environment. Growing up in a community like that, attending a high school like that made me realize that the rest of the world existed and that we could all live together. Everybody had Caucasian friends, Mexican friends, black friends, it didn't matter. It wasn't a utopia — there was racial tension and trouble, but we were all thrown together and had to figure out how to make it work. In the Midwest and other parts of the country, I've seen kids entering college before they ever are really brought face to face with another culture; that could never happen in California, which remains a genuine melting pot.

By the same token, the "melting pot" is the source of some of California's problems, and the problems people have adjusting to California life. People go there with all these romantic Golden Gate visions, and then they find it's a real struggle to exist there economically. That's always been the case, and the competition for limited resources is at the heart of many of the racial and ethnic tensions that do exist there. People go to California and encounter this struggle, and they don't always turn out to be as friendly and cosmopolitan as they'd hoped to be.

But I think there's more acceptance across racial lines, just because the racial and ethnic variety is so much a part of life. There are Asians and Hispanics, blacks and Caucasians, all intermingled. The cities haven't been planned out like inner cities in older parts of the country, people just live anywhere. Clearly, California has the same problems as anywhere, but it's starting from a different, a healthier base.

Of course, I never gave a thought to the politics of it then. I just knew that, growing up in Southern California in the 1950s, I was a half-hour from the mountains, 50 minutes from the beach, an hour from Los Angeles, two hours from San Diego, and 2 1/2 hours from Tijuana, Mexico. The whole area was a playground, and I spent some time in all of those places during high school.

In 11th grade, I bought my first car. You have to understand, I didn't have a lot of money, but it was a simple rule in Southern California in 1959: if you didn't own a car, you didn't exist as a human being. I bought a 1950 Ford coupe for $200. If you really wanted to fit in the car scene, you had to put your car on a rake, meaning that the front end was lowered and the back end was jacked up high. You also had to paint the undercarriage of your car white. I did the paint job myself, and I have to tell you it looked awfully stupid. But boy, was I proud of it. Then, of course, you had to install the mandatory glass-pack mufflers to make it sound like a dragster. You couldn't have a car that sounded like the family station wagon. It had to be loud, man, loud. Yeah, I felt pretty hot cruising town in my '50 Ford.

I helped form a car club, the Lifters. That was another reality of the time and place, the car club. I had a little metal plaque I put in my back window, "The Lifters." Not that we ever really *did* anything as a club, mind you. None of us had any money, so we'd meet once in a while and talk about cars, and that was about it. Then we'd go "cruising," the great Southern California teen sport, just driving your car aimlessly around. If you've seen *American Graffiti*, you know what I mean. That movie was my life, in uncanny detail.

Senior prom was a memorable night. A neighbor and I loaded up dozens of big boulders and carted them down into his basement. With the boulders and a water pump, we built a big fountain, and we turned his basement into a restaurant. We hired his brother to be the waiter, and somehow we talked his parents into fixing us a steak dinner. Then we paid a couple of guys to take our cars and pick up our dates. When the "chauffeured limousines" returned with the girls, we met them at the curb and escorted them into our classy restaurant, Johnny Mathis singing "The Twelfth of Never" on the stereo. What a couple of smoothies we pictured ourselves. After the prom, we went to see Connie Francis in *Where the Boys Are*.

My first job was pure Southern California, too, but an element of Southern California that has become pure Americana, exported to the world. There was a house up on the mountain behind our house where a couple of brothers lived for years. Their name was McDonald, and they had started a diner in the Los Angeles area in the 1940s, relocating to San Bernardino in the early '50s. There they spun off of the diner concept and introduced something new in dining: fast food.

People in Des Plaines, Illinois, claim to have the first McDonald's, but what they have there is the first franchised McDonald's owned by Ray Kroc. The original McDonald's fast-food restaurant, owned by the McDonald brothers, was in San Bernardino, California, two blocks from my high school. We went there when I was a little kid. I remember my dad piling us all in the car and heading to McDonald's. There was no inside seating, you'd park outdoors and walk in and order your food at a counter. It was a small building set underneath two enormous golden arches.

McDonald's was a hot spot in San Bernardino. Everyone went to buy these cheap, quick burgers, a whole new concept. Hamburgers were 15 cents, and they were just like what you buy at McDonald's anywhere in the world today. There were cheeseburgers, french fries were 12 cents, milk shakes were a dime. If you got a red star on your receipt, then whatever you had ordered was free. I remember the Hebert family loading up on burgers and fries one time and drawing the red star — that was a big night.

I got a part-time job there in 1958, and I learned how to fry burgers, how to measure and weigh ice cream into the milk shake cups, how to dump the fries. I had no idea what a part of history I was involved with. One of my other jobs was to get on the ladder outside the restaurant and change the numbers on the billboard out front. Where today the sign at every McDonald's in the world says, "Billions and Billions Served," back in 1958, we kept an accurate tally. "We have sold 200,000 hamburgers." Maybe six weeks later, I'd be up on the ladder again: "We have sold 225,000 hamburgers."

One day we got new milkshake machines. I remember it because one of the jobs I hated was scooping the ice cream from big containers into cups. We stored hundreds of cups full of ice cream so that we could serve people quickly with the right amount of ice cream already measured. When someone would order a shake, you'd grab one of these cups, add the flavoring and the milk and stick it on the machine.

Then this milkshake machine distributor came along with a new machine with four mixers that made the job a breeze. That was Ray Kroc, and that's how he met the McDonald brothers. He became partners with them and eventually he bought them out, and the rest is burger history. Kroc became Mr. Hamburger. And I used his original milk shake machine. Now I take my volleyball teams to places like Yugoslavia and we see a McDonald's in the middle of Zagreb.

So that was life during high school — sports, burgers, cruising. I just cruised in the classroom, too. I got pretty good grades, but I never had to put too much effort into it, and probably because of that, I didn't have any more idea where I was going in my life than I did when I was driving around in my Ford.

I was offered a scholarship to Connecticut Wesleyan to play basketball. My mother had a friend who had attended Connecticut Wesleyan and lived in Redlands, not far from San Bernardino. Redlands High School was in our conference, the Citrus Belt League. My mom's friend knew the coach at Redlands, a guy named Jerry Tarkanian. That's right, another high school brush with greatness — I played against teams coached by Tark the Shark.

The Connecticut Wesleyan grad invited me to have dinner at Tarkanian's house with Danny Wolthers, a Redlands player who eventually ended up attending Cal-Berkeley. The idea behind the dinner was to talk about our future in college basketball and convince us that Connecticut Wesleyan was the place for us. The whole thing fell through, though, and I didn't take advantage of the scholarship offer.

For one thing, Connecticut seemed like the other side of the world. For another, basketball really wasn't that big a deal to me. At that point in my life, I didn't have much focus. I didn't have a clue what I wanted to do. No one in my family knew much about selecting a college, either. My mother had a high school education, and there was just nobody around to provide us with any direction. I was just hanging out and not really thinking about my future. So in the fall of 1961, when the time came to make one of the most important decisions in my life, I put about as much thought into the choice as I would deciding between a hamburger and a cheeseburger at McDonald's.

CHAPTER 2

NET GAIN

I had some friends down the block who were Mormons, and they were going to Brigham Young, and I just more or less said, "Sure, I'll go there, too." When we got there, I had no idea what I wanted to do, where to go, what to study. My friend wanted to be an engineer, so I stood in line with him and registered as a freshman engineering student. They gave me a schedule, and I just said, "Oh, OK." I was so naive, so sheltered, I had no idea what was happening.

I started to realize I'd taken a wrong turn when I was sitting in chemistry and math classes with no concept of what they were trying to teach me, completely lost. That showed up in my first-semester grades, and at that point I finally had enough sense to switch into some courses in the social sciences. I made out a little better the second semester.

Still, I was a fish out of water in Provo, Utah. It was bad enough I wasn't a Mormon, but I was a Californian to boot. I didn't understand how all-encompassing the Mormon culture is in Utah. Brigham Young only allowed five percent of its college community to be non-Mormon. I was back to being an outsider. I made some friends and enjoyed the scenery — the Wasatch Mountains north of Provo are beautiful — but I clearly didn't belong.

I had to take a Mormon religion class, and among the nuggets of wisdom our instructor presented to us was that non-whites were given their dark complexions as a punishment for sins of their ancestors, and that as a result none could hold high office in the church. I may have been pretty naive, but I could recognize racism when I was banged over the head with it. Four years of this sort of indoctrination just wasn't going to wash.

One day in the spring of 1962, I was on the phone with a close friend from San Bernardino named Stan Orrock, who was going to Cal-Santa Barbara. He knew I was getting by at BYU, but he also knew I wasn't really happy there.

"What are you doing all the way out there in Utah?" he said finally. I thought about it a minute. "You're right," I said, "what *am* I doing here?" I may not have had much more direction in going to UCSB than I had in going to BYU, but at least now I knew where I *didn't* want to be. During the summer, I worked out a transfer and headed to Santa Barbara for my sophomore year. And even if I didn't have much of a plan in the fall of '62, there was something waiting for me back in California that would eventually give me a direction in life.

When I arrived on campus, Stan immediately started trying to sell me on joining his fraternity, Sigma Phi Epsilon. "You'll love it," he told me. "Hey, we've got a V-ball court on the side of the fraternity house." We'd been basketball teammates at San Bernardino High, and when he said "V-ball," I heard "B-ball." I didn't have any notion of volleyball being a big deal. I joined the Sig Eps with visions of this great basketball court at the fraternity.

First thing when I got to the house, I looked out the window and was really confused. I saw a sand court with a net strung across it. "That's the V-ball court," Stan told me. It didn't take me long to learn that volleyball was part of the culture in Santa Barbara. You just play volleyball, it's not even questioned. It's an art form, a religion.

Volleyball was invented in the United States late in the 19th century and was spread around the world by the U.S. Armed Forces. In the years after World War II, the rest of the world passed up the U.S. in volleyball proficiency, and the Americans really didn't catch up again until the late 1970s.

For a long time there were only small pockets of volleyball fanatics in New York and Chicago and Philadelphia and other cities around the country. California, though, had something the other cities lacked: enormous stretches of undeveloped beach. California's YMCA players took volleyball to the beach in the '50s, and once it reached the beach, a select system of rules evolved around the doubles game, and an entire subculture of beach volleyball began to emerge.

Net Gain 15

The beach volleyball culture in California developed up and down the coastline of Southern California, including the state beach at Santa Monica, Hermosa Beach, Redondo Beach, and Manhattan Beach. The South Bay is the cradle of volleyball in the United States and, along with Hawaii, kept the sport alive during the lean years from the late 1940s to the '60s. Eventually this group of beach players brought the game back indoors and formed six-man teams. These six-man indoor teams played in U.S. Volleyball Association tournaments and fostered interest in the game.

The club volleyball movement at colleges such as UCLA, San Jose State, Cal, Cal-Santa Barbara, San Diego State and Southern Cal got started when these beach players went to college in the mid- to late 1950s. These V-ball pioneers played year-round, competing on the beach during the summer and moving indoors in the late fall.

As the club volleyball movement began to grow and mature in the late 1950s and early '60s, the California athletic departments began to adopt these club teams as varsity men's programs. It was the beginning of the college game and I was right in the middle of it. I had no idea at the time, but I was there for the renaissance of the game in the United States.

There were relatively few women volleyball players in the 1960s and early '70s. The U.S. national team was a collection of all-stars thrown together at the last minute to play in international competitions. The Eastern European countries took women's volleyball very seriously in the mid- to late 1960s, but it was the Japanese national teams in 1964 and 1968 that really spurred interest in women's volleyball. Japan expanded the awareness that women could play world-class volleyball. The Japanese won the gold medal in the '64 Olympics in Tokyo, and suddenly the sport was legitimized for women. Since the 1968 Games, the women's game has continued to improve dramatically, and in a way everything we're trying to do at Illinois in the '90s owes a debt to those early Japanese teams.

But however far volleyball has come in the last third of a century, the California game has never lost its beach roots. For a lot of players, volleyball *is* beach volleyball, and in the early '60s, Santa Barbara was one of the sport's meccas. At Isla Vista, the UCSB student ghetto right next to campus, you couldn't drive two blocks without seeing dozens of sand volleyball courts next to apartment buildings, fraternities and sororities, every living space. A building wasn't considered habitable without a court. Then a few blocks away was the beach, and it was completely strung with volleyball courts.

So here I was in Isla Vista in the fall of 1962, and in no time I fell in love with the sand volleyball game. It was a pretty simple routine: get up, go to the beach, set up a net and play. Check your watch, and if it was time for a class, you'd brush the sand off, throw on a T-shirt and head over to campus for an hour. Get out of class, back to the beach for some more volleyball. I remember going down to the beach at 8, 8:30 in the morning, setting up a net and playing until 8 or 9 at night, with just enough breaks to fit in classes and maybe a meal or two.

And when you learn the game, you learn The System. Again, very simple: when your team shows up at the court, you put your names at the bottom of the challenge list. The winners hold the court as long as they win. When your turn comes, if you win, the court is yours and the next challenger comes up. Lose, and you either move to another court or put your names back at the bottom of the list. It's like the Code of the West: you live by The System, and you never question it.

I played every day on the beach, then took my game indoors. When I came to Santa Barbara in 1962, there was no such thing as a varsity collegiate volleyball program anywhere in California, but club volleyball was at its height. I made the UCSB men's club volleyball team in the fall of 1963, my introduction to six-man indoor volleyball. We played UCLA, Cal, San Jose State and all of the university club teams in California. You might wonder what the difference is between top-flight club sports and varsity sports. Well, this should give you an idea: we had to raise money and go down to the YMCA to buy matching gym shorts so we would all look alike. We each got one pair of shorts and one matching short-sleeve jersey, and that was rare at the time. I graduated in January of 1966, and the school made the club team a varsity program the following fall. I was on the last club team.

We had some pretty decent players come through UCSB, and it seems like half of them went on to become coaches. Oregon's Gerald Gregory was a Gaucho, and so were Don Shaw at Stanford, Hawaii's Dave Shoji and Tom Shoji, formerly at Indiana, just to name a few. A few years ago, I was at an elite volleyball camp in Colorado and several coaches were comparing notes when we realized how many of us had been at UCSB. Some of the camp organizers went out and bought us "Ex-Gaucho" T-shirts, and we played the rest of the staff in an exhibition match — we had Dave Shoji as setter, Gerry Gregory the middle hitter, Kenny Preston, the men's coach at UCSB — just a great all-star, all-Gaucho team.

The only one of those guys I went to school with was Dave Shoji, who was a freshman when I was a senior. I got to watch him learn how to play volleyball that year just like I'd learned a couple of years before. By that time, I was pretty well known as a volleyball player on campus. I had a 36-inch vertical jump, I was quick, could hit the ball pretty hard, and was a good defensive player. The last time we were in Honolulu, I heard Dave say in an interview that I was one of the best players at UCSB when he was in school and that he had looked up to me and learned the game from me and several of the other players. That was a gratifying moment.

We were pretty good and the volleyball was intense. As you can imagine, Santa Barbara gave the team enormous support. I remember playing UCLA one night in the fall of 1964 when we had more than 4,000 fans turn out to see the match. It was right after the '64 Tokyo Olympics, and volleyball had been introduced as an Olympic sport that year. Three U.S. players had returned to college and were playing for UCLA. The players from both teams headed to a bar after the match to listen to stories from the Olympians about the Games. I can still see myself sitting at Lou's Bar and Grill in Goleta, listening to Ernie Suwara, an Olympic starter. He had all of us spellbound.

It was tough for that first U.S. Olympic team. As the sport had evolved in America, the rules were naturally influenced by the beach game, but there were important differences, and the international rules differed from both versions Americans were familiar with. On the beach, there were very rigid rules about ball handling. Everything had to be received underhand, even setting. In the American indoor game, on the other hand, serves could be received overhanded. Everyone could block, all six players could rush the net. A team could screen for the server — we'd line up and our server would hit the ball from behind this blind wall. We also used to clap in unison every time one of our players would receive the ball overhand so the referee couldn't hear whether the ball had been lifted or not — that was just how the game was played at the time.

The rules were evolving throughout the early '60s. Referees' ball handling calls were very rigid. You had to set the ball straight ahead, for example — no side-setting or spin-setting was allowed. The players and referees were creating a distinctly American form of the game. At the same time, though, the development of the American game hamstrung our teams in early international competition. The game had evolved in such a cloister in California that no one realized how different the game was around the world.

Ernie told us that night how the U.S. team got smoked in its early Olympic matches, largely because they were essentially playing by the wrong rules. They were receiving serves overhanded and were being whistled every time. The Americans' ball handling techniques were completely alien to the international rules structure. Finally they held some team meetings to try and figure out how to play this suddenly exotic game. They adapted to the international referees, and they became more competitive. The 1964 Olympics was a vital learning experience for our national team, and now, just three or four weeks after the Games, Ernie and some of his teammates were passing the lesson along to us. We were among the first to hear about the future of volleyball in our country.

A year later, the Cal-Santa Barbara team went to the U.S. Volleyball Association Collegiate Division national tournament in Omaha, Nebraska. Since there weren't varsity programs yet, this was our equivalent of the NCAA tournament. A team from Mexico drove up for the tourney, a tremendous team. They had ridden up on a bus, along with their fans — you can imagine what a big trip it was for them. These players were setting the ball away from their body lines, creating new and different angles — they were, in short, playing the international-style game — and they were being whistled by the American referees every time they touched the ball. They couldn't speak English, and they had no idea what was going on; they got hammered, even though it was a very good team. It was the '64 U.S. team's Olympic experience in reverse, and it showed again that the American style and the international style needed to get in step.

For many years in America, blockers couldn't penetrate the net. Teams were just whaling away on the ball, while the blocker's hands had to remain on his own side of the net. That rule changed in the mid-1960s. Another outdated blocking rule

Net Gain 19

was that the block counted as a contact. After a block, all you had left was set, then hit. Following the 1968 Olympics, the international volleyball governing body changed the rule so that a block no longer counts as an initial contact.

Even the ball was different in America. We used a leather ball, similar to the beach volleyball used today, 12 or 18 patches sewn together. In 1965, right after the Olympics, the uniconstruction ball was introduced to the indoor game, and that became one more adjustment the California game had to make to adapt to the international style.

I was playing volleyball throughout these rule changes, so I got to observe the evolution up close. One change I didn't get to take advantage of was the way top volleyball players have come to be remunerated. I played on the beach for about three years with Gene Tyworth, who is now a professor at Penn State. If we won a tournament, we'd get an eight-inch plastic trophy and maybe a free hamburger at some restaurant. Today, Karch Kiraly and other beach players are millionaires. The game was a passion for us, sure, but nobody could have foreseen that you could make a fortune at something that most of us took up as a diversion between classes.

Oh, yeah, classes. Contrary to what you might think from what you've read so far, I did go to classes, and I didn't do too badly, considering the distractions. Just like at BYU, I started out with no real plan, enrolling in liberal arts, like everybody else who didn't have a plan. My academic advisor, a guy named Tomatso Shibutanti, was a sociology professor, and his classes were captivating. He would walk into class, never had a note, a book, nothing, and he would deliver, nonstop, the most amazing lectures. This guy would get an ovation after every one of his lectures, he was so brilliant. I'd never seen anything like it, and so, naturally, I majored in sociology.

Two courses I took as a sophomore taught me an awful lot about the world, and a lot of it didn't gibe with what I'd been taught at St. Bernardine's. In physical anthropology, I read Darwin for the first time and got an understanding of the theory of natural selection. It was such a new and exciting set of ideas to me that I read everything else about it I could get my hands on. It was the first time I'd had creation called into question, and it made me wonder about the whole religious system underlying creationism.

Then I took an introductory world history course, and for the first time, Jesus was presented to me as a historical figure, somebody who did these things, lived during these times, said these things, but was one among a series of people who've had a similar impact on the human race. I learned the history of theism and began to appreciate the economic and social roots underlying the various forms of organized religion. The biggest lesson I took from these two classes is that intellectual life, social life, moral life all require that you delve into the mysteries for yourself rather than accepting conventional wisdom — in short, that you "question authority."

But I'm making myself out to be some deep thinker at age 20. I learned some things, yes — and to a great extent learned *how* to learn things, how to think for myself — but remember, I was in Santa Barbara. How seriously could you really take academics at Santa Barbara? What a campus. Class, beach, volleyball, not necessarily in that order.

I took my wife, Sherry, to Isla Vista a few years ago. She didn't say a word during our entire trip. Finally, when I asked what was wrong, she replied, "I'm just so angry that somebody can go to college in a place like this. It is a paradise." She's right. Santa Barbara is one of the neatest places in the world. The campus is right on the beach. I took a ceramics class, and the ceramics studio was right on a beautiful lagoon jutting in from the ocean. I recall sitting in class, throwing pots and looking out at the Pacific. I still have some of the pieces I made in that class.

Santa Barbara's a University of California campus, so you had to be in at least the top 10 percent of your class to get in, so it's not like the place was populated with a bunch of dummies. Still, it was a remarkable party atmosphere. Everyone I've ever talked to who went to UCSB tells the same story: we learned after just a few months out of school that you can't say much about your college days because people just won't believe it. They think you're making up all these stories of oceanside paradise. We thought this was what college was like, one big party, like being on a beautiful vacation. But when there's a group of people telling college stories and someone from Santa Barbara starts in, the other people just roll their eyes. So we've learned to keep our idyllic memories to ourselves. Of course, having gone to college in a bubble, we all had a lot of adjustments to make when we were thrown out into the real world.

Net Gain

If *American Graffiti* was a chronicle of my high school life, my college career once I returned to California was *Animal House*, crazed fraternity life. It was uncanny, right down to motorcycling up the stairs at the house. I mean, I'm talking about some dopey stunts. In my junior year, my roommate Keith Morden decided he wanted to be a cheerleader, so he talked some of us into going to the tryouts to root for him. Naturally, you have to prepare for an event like this, so we sat around all day drinking beer. By the time the tryouts started, we had to help Keith on stage. Then, continuing our unselfish support, we started yelling cheers along with him during his tryout. Apparently, the people responsible for the selection process were as loopy as we were: a few hours later, we found out we'd been elected as a four-man cheerleading squad.

Of course, cheerleading wasn't as regimented in those days. One guy had a microphone, and it was all ad lib. We just went to the game and made things up as we went along. One day, for example, our mighty Gauchos football team was playing Long Beach State and I led a cheer, "Forty-Niners, Eat Your Nuggets." The cheer was roundly booed, which we took as a compliment.

A few weeks later, the football team was headed for Cal Poly, and our little squad didn't have enough money to make the 100-mile trip to San Luis Obispo. We hopped on a bus with the COGS, the Campus Organization for Gaucho Spirit. We were having a fine time building spirit on the chartered bus — in fact, they had brought along five kegs of spirit — until midway through the trip, the bus was stopped because several COGS members had raided a convenience store. We weren't involved, so the police let the cheerleading squad leave. We headed for the railroad yard and hopped a box car, but a railroad security cop chased us off the train at Guadalupe, still about 25 miles out of San Luis Obispo. Finally we ended up hitchhiking, arriving in the second quarter of the game.

We were on our way in when Mark Israel tumbled over a low fence and passed out. We presented a fine image of our university: three cheerleaders covered with dirt and a fourth one unconscious over a railing in front of the stands. During a timeout, we headed over to the Cal Poly side of the field and captured their mascot. We did unspeakable things to the mascot and the fans booed us to death, just the reaction we'd hoped for.

When we got back to campus, the student body president informed me that Cal Poly's president — the university president, mind you, not just the student body president — had registered a complaint about our behavior at the game. Some people just have no sense of humor, I guess. That was the end of my short-lived cheerleading career. Later that week, after a student council meeting, the school paper headlines read, "Cheerleaders Ousted in Spirit Clean-up." I still have the newspaper on my desk.

We didn't take anything seriously at Sigma Phi Epsilon. Before my senior year, we read in the student newspaper how something had gotten screwed up in the student class elections. A guy named Frank Seelinbinder had won the election for senior class president, but because of some procedural snafu, the vote was voided, necessitating a new election.

It didn't take us long to determine the appropriate course of action. Substituting a beer-filled beach for the traditional smoke-filled room, the fraternity decided it would launch a couple of political careers with a write-in campaign in the new election: Mike Hebert for president, Mike Sullivan for vice president. We thought it would be a great gag on campus, the Hebert-Sullivan ticket. People canvassed the campus handing out leaflets boosting this bogus campaign. Our names were everywhere. Well, I think it was Lincoln who said you can fool all of the people some of the time. This poor sap Seelinbinder, the duly elected class president, ran smack into a fraternity prank. The Hebert-Sullivan write-in ticket won the election, and I was the senior class president. I honestly don't remember a single thing I did to exercise my executive authority.

That was the extent of my political involvement. Otherwise, it was life on the beach as usual. The great simmering issues of the time — civil rights, feminism, the free speech movement — I just wasn't paying much attention. I was at UCSB in 1964 when the very first student demonstration took place at Cal-Berkeley. Mario Savio, a student at Berkeley, was the leader of the free speech movement, the FSM. I remember my sociology instructor coming to class one day distraught over what was happening to Savio at Berkeley. He was what we called "a Berkeley type" — New York accent, wore a suit to class — a *suit!* At *UCSB!* — and he was a good friend and associate of Savio's. He was a bright, articulate young guy, and he spent some time trying to explain to us what this free speech movement at Berkeley was all about.

Unfortunately, he was talking to a bunch of Santa Barbara beach boys who were antsy to get back to the volleyball courts. Eventually, I realized that this guy was at the forefront of the whole college student movement. The roots of the protests all across the country in the '60s were in the FSM at Berkeley. But it would be a while before I'd understand that — or care. I still had a lot of growing up to do, and for that to happen, I had to drag myself away from the beach and see a little more of the world.

SCIENCE ALFRESCO

In my senior year at Santa Barbara, I applied for the Peace Corps. The program had been started by President Kennedy in the early 1960s, and I had thought about it for some time. The notion of helping people and at the same time expanding my horizons was attractive. Kennedy had been killed while I was in school, and the carefree Santa Barbara life was starting to fade. Like a lot of people in my generation, I'd begun a process of evolution — from baby-boomer optimism to '60s radicalism. Then too, I wanted to test myself. I'd gained a lot of self-confidence during my college years, but I wasn't sure how much of that was genuine and how much was dependent on the Cal-Santa Barbara environment. Could I make it on my own?

I wasn't on the front lines of the antiwar movement in 1965, but I knew I didn't want to go into the military. Military service had already left a painful and indelible mark on my family. By the same token, I didn't want to be seen — by others or by myself — as someone who just wanted a free ride. In 1965, the Peace Corps qualified as "alternate service" in lieu of military obligation. Between the time I applied and my graduation in January 1966, Congress ended the Peace Corps' alternate service status, but I wanted to go regardless. I was immediately assigned to a three-month Nigeria training program at UCLA, starting with a month working with families in the Watts section of Los Angeles. This was just months after the riots in the summer of 1965, one of the worst eruptions of racial strife in our country's history, and the community was still smoldering. Out of 104 recruits headed for Africa, all but two of us were white, and almost everyone was middle-class. The Peace Corps' plan, I guess, was to acclimate us with living in a black community, and to give us a sense of the deprivation of the Third World.

They bused us out to Watts, where our host families met us. Then we were on our own. Overnight, I went from my Bohemian college environment to one of the political hotbeds of the nation. There were still charred timbers from buildings that had been burned, and there were still people roaming the streets. There was tension, suspicion of any white face. We weren't bused back at the end of the day, either. We spent all of our time in Watts — we lived there, ate there, worked there. It wasn't always comfortable, being the minority — and that, of course, was exactly the point: to turn the tables on my comfortable Isla Vista experience, to drag me off of the beach once and for all. I gained a great deal personally from that immersion in a culture so completely different from mine. I also developed sensitivities and insights that I might never have gained otherwise.

After a month in Watts, it was back to UCLA for language training, and the next thing I knew I was getting off a plane in Lagos, Nigeria. This is it, beach boy — this is no vacation, this is life. Isla Vista to Nigeria — it was like jumping from a Jacuzzi into a pool of ice water. There's always been a side of me that hungers for that type of shock to the system, and it was time to feed that hunger.

In the Peace Corps, volunteers are sent out individually into the villages and cities. It's not like a military setting, where you're in barracks. There is no one to go back to at night and say, "Wow, here's what I did today," and to know that person will understand what you're talking about because you share a cultural background. Each volunteer is entirely on his own to encounter and assimilate a culture 5,000 miles, 10,000 miles from home. When we were in our first orientation session in Enugu, a Nigerian man, one of the local Peace Corps administrators, sat down next to me and held my hand. Coming from a culture where such a gesture between men was considered inappropriate, I froze, not knowing how to react. He held my hand for the entire meeting. I learned later that in this part of West Africa, men hold hands as a gesture of friendship, with no sexual connotation whatever.

There were about 80 of us in the orientation program in Enugu. During the day, we would teach or learn about the language and culture. At night, everyone would go exploring in the city. Within a few days, everyone came down with dysentery. Somehow I managed to escape that scourge, along with three other guys I hung out with. We would sneak out after lights out and hit the bars and explore the alleys and the back streets. It seemed like we were the only four volunteers who weren't doubled over with dysentery or some virus. Maybe the beer built up our resistance.

I was assigned to St. John's Teachers College in Diobu, a village outside of Port Harcourt. Port Harcourt is on the Niger River delta, a few miles inland from the Atlantic Ocean and just 300 miles north of the equator. St. John's had been built in the 1930s as a teacher training college, part of the educational system developed during British colonial rule. The headmaster was an Englishman, and all of the instructors were Nigerian except for the one volunteer position. My predecessor was a Canadian woman, and the headmaster, surprised to see a man as the volunteer's replacement, had to scramble to find me appropriate living quarters.

He put me in a hut on the compound of the college. The buildings on the compound were a pastiche of stucco, cinderblock, and adobe, with corrugated tin roofs. There were no glass windows, just screens with maybe a half-inch mesh, designed to keep the bigger animals out.

My first night in the hut, I was kept awake by a goat that was tied to a tree outside. The next morning I showed one of the teachers the goat and asked what could be done about it. The tree the goat was tied to, it turned out, was an iroko, sacred in one of the village medicine man's ju-ju rites. To the California boy, the goat was just a noisy nuisance, but to the villagers, he was part of an ancient ritual, tied up as a sacrifice to appease the gods. There was no moving the goat.

There are three levels of higher education in Nigeria. St. John's was a Level 2 training center, designed to prepare Nigerian teachers to work in elementary schools, teaching reading, writing, math and science. I had gotten a D in my college biology class, so naturally, given the way bureaucracies work, I was assigned to teach science. My job was to equip these students with enough scientific background to handle teaching a grade school science class.

The educational system was much like ours — semesters, lesson plans, grade books, exams — but my class of teacher trainees was made up entirely of men, ranging in age from 18 to

55. The range of their backgrounds was just as broad: some came from families that had lived in small villages forever, and they still wore authentic tribal clothing; others lived in cities and wore slacks and polo shirts. When I arrived at St. John's, the headmaster greeted me with the news that there was no science room, no science equipment, no science curriculum. I had to put together a science class from scratch. First, we converted half of the student lounge to a science room. A local mason helped me wall off the area. Then I found a carpenter who thought he could make the furniture we'd need. He and I designed lab tables, stools and a blackboard. I bought a UNESCO Science Resource Book so we could make some rudimentary lab equipment.

I didn't know anything about science, but that didn't matter, because the science I had to teach was the science that we learn from watching commercials on TV. Some of the most basic concepts were new to my students. One of their favorite experiments involved electrical circuitry, building a circuit with wire, batteries and a light bulb. Then I had them build the circuit except for a three-inch gap between two nails. They would put various items across the gap to see which ones would complete the circuit and light the bulb, and which ones would fail. They were learning about conductivity, an entirely new concept.

We also built a scale out of balsa wood, jar tops, a razor blade and a coat hanger. Once the scale was constructed, we had to find a standard measure of weight. Pounds or kilograms didn't mean anything — things weighed the equivalent of two grapefruits, or six oranges. The scale taught valuable lessons in weight relationships. The students were amazed that a quantity of water weighed the same as seven walnuts. They had never thought of a liquid having weight at all. The fact that some water could weigh more than a walnut was another completely new concept.

These were not stupid people, they just grew up in a different culture, a culture with different demands. They were far more comfortable with spatial relationships than we were, for example. One day, another volunteer and I were walking through a marketplace and he decided to conduct an experiment. He had a jar and asked people to guess how many cups of rice would fit in the jar. Our own guesses weren't even close, but the people in the marketplace, independent of each other, all guessed 14 1/2 or 15, which was correct. All of the people who came by could see the spatial relationship between that jar and this cup immediately. They had grown up in a culture that rewards spatial judgments. A person can't thrive in the marketplace without a keen sense of how much of a commodity he's paying for.

Sometimes I'd almost regret having to change the more poetic way they had of looking at things. We talked about air one day, how air is present everywhere and how air pressure can cause different weather, how we breathe oxygen that's in the air. I looked out the window and saw the wind blowing a tree. "What's happening out there?" I asked. A man raised his hand: "The tree is dancing!" From their cultural perspective, every-thing is animate, it's a world of music, dance, rhythm. The tree was dancing.

"No," I had to say, "it's because the wind is being pushed by atmospheric conditions and the tree gets in the way, and the wind encounters the leaves and branches," and so on and so forth, blah, blah, blah. What a drab explanation, compared with, "The tree is dancing."

English is the official language in Nigeria, but there are 52 Nigerian dialects and tribal languages. Many people also speak pidgin English, which is supposedly similar to the Cajun dialect in the Louisiana bayou. I couldn't say for sure — I didn't understand a word of pidgin English, but then my father's family is Cajun, and I don't understand a word of that, either.

I learned Ibo, one of the three most common dialects. Ibo is a tonal language — the tone of each syllable contributes to the meaning of each word. Take the word "akwa" — if I say "AK-wa," high-low, that means "egg," but if I say "ak-WA," low-high, that means "door." Sentences begin with a high tone and end with a low tone, and the speech is very melodic.

In my experience, the English spoken in black communi-ties is much more melodic and loud than what whites typically speak, and I wonder whether that's not connected to African roots. Language in Africa is not just communication, it's song. The two linguists, Bill and Bea Wellmers, who had trained us at UCLA had just returned from field study in Nigeria, and they had committed the language to writing for the first time, prepar-ing a grammar workbook. A Nigerian assistant who was in-volved in the training saw the book and was just awed. This was a college-educated man who'd studied English and French in books, but this was the first time he'd seen his native language presented as a subject for academic study, just like those other languages. It assigned a new credibility to his language, and that filled him with pride.

My first day of class, armed with my rudimentary knowledge of Ibo, I began reading the class roster and was just lost. "Ezawekwe Ofikwo . . . Odomeus Obakeke . . ." I know I must have been murdering the names. In an American classroom, of course, the students would have been rolling in the aisles, but the concept of laughing at an instructor, or of showing any kind of disrespect, was foreign to these students. They sat at attention at all times, always addressing me as "sir." Even after I got to know them, the classroom remained a formal place. Too formal for me, in fact, but I knew *I* had to honor their tradition of respect.

My teaching didn't end in the classroom, either. I realized I'd hardly be bringing my students the best of American civilization if I didn't teach them sports. Actually, I think teaching them basketball and volleyball may have been a defense mechanism, so that I wouldn't have to play their sport, soccer. I was hopeless at soccer, far worse than their lowest level pickup games.

The same local carpenter who had helped me build the science lab pitched in to build volleyball standards and basketball "rings," and a local fisherman wove the basketball and volleyball nets. The basketball net presented a problem, though. The fisherman's first effort was a straight cylinder, and the ball would fall through without slowing down.

I'd try to explain, "No, at the bottom it's got to have a little tension, so it just catches the ball for a moment, then lets it go." He never quite got it. Unfortunately, Ibo has no word for "swish." There also weren't any patches of asphalt handy, so some of the local people cleared away some land for a court. Sometime I'd wake up to the sound of their machetes. It sounded sort of like a chain gang — whack! whack! — except that their rhythmic singing was so joyful.

Teaching basketball was tricky. Since the Nigerians' sport was soccer, they rebelled at the notion of using their hands. Dribbling was particularly comical to them; when I tried to demonstrate, they just laughed at me, thought I was crazy. They would kick the ball around, but they wouldn't dribble it. Finally they got the idea to shoot it, or rather to fling it at the backboard. Well, it was a start.

Inevitably, after a few aimless heaves at the backboard, someone actually would get the ball to fall through the hoop. That would prompt a wild soccer-style celebration, the shooter running around with his fist in the air, everyone shouting "goal, goal!" Finally the other players would mob the shooter in a group hug, sending him sprawling backwards onto the ground. It was hilarious, maybe even as hilarious as I was to them when I tried to play soccer.

It was the same when I tried to teach them volleyball. When someone would knock down a spike or get a serve over the net, the game would disintegrate into a wild celebration. The concept of continuous play was a tough one to convey.

I found a group of foreign pick-up volleyball players at a local sports club. There were about eight of us at one time or another. The ringleader was from a Dutch oil company — he had the volleyball. There was the Dutchman, a guy named Antonio, who was our setter, John Brown from Cornell, who was a Peace Corps volunteer, and Salem.

Salem was a Lebanese jukebox distributor in Port Harcourt. He was like a character in a movie, just driving around delivering jukeboxes out of his pickup truck. Salem was a piece of work. He always had jewels on his fingers and around his neck, and he always had plenty of cash. Salem would show up for a volleyball game with a gorgeous woman on each arm, all decked out in tight dresses. Was he a pimp? Some kind of wheeler-dealer? I don't know, but Salem had something going on, that's for certain.

On weekends, this group would get together with our new rubber Voit AMF outdoor volleyball and head to some other town to play a game. I got the Voit from a guy I knew in the USAID office, the Agency for International Development. A lot of people were convinced USAID was a front for CIA operations; it might have been, but they got us a volleyball. There were probably three volleyball teams in the entire country of Nigeria, and we had two volleyballs.

There were four or five Peace Corps volunteers who lived within 50 miles of each other, and we set up a fantasy basketball league. It wasn't a one-on-one game in the traditional sense. The way it worked was, you called a shot appropriate for a player on your team. The idea was to mimic the pros' styles. I was the Boston Celtics, so, for example, if I called "Sam Jones," I had to hit his bank shot from the side. If I called "K.C. Jones," I had to launch one from the top of the circle, and so on, with "Russell" and "Havlicek," everybody on the team. You had to distribute your shots among your players, it couldn't just be a fast-break lay-up every time down the floor.

It was an eight-quarter game, each player shooting 10 shots per quarter. You added up your points at the end of each quarter, and the winner of the quarter got three one-and-one free throw opportunities. We kept track of all the statistics for each player. We kept league scoring averages, league standings, had an annual all-star game. I guess you could say we had some time on our hands.

I remember the league's big controversy, the Dick Barnett scoring title. A guy from Long Island, a pretty good player, was the Knicks. Every time he really needed a hoop, he went to Dick Barnett. The rest of us, here we are shooting Bill Russell hooks, Dolph Schayes two-hand set shots from 30 feet, whatever, and this guy's standing on the perimeter popping Dick Barnett jumpers. Where's the commissioner when you need him?

CHAPTER 4

TEACHING, LEARNING

Our basketball games were frivolous, sure, but they were also a way of keeping a link to home. It's a hard environment to deal with for someone coming from privileged America, even my segment of America, which I hadn't thought was all that privileged. Now you're using kerosene lamps. A shower is a bucket of water you've heated over a fire you built, hung on a hook upstairs; you stand under a spigot you've welded under the bucket, and it lasts about 30 seconds if you're lucky. That's it — back to real life, Nigeria style.

The Peace Corps did furnish every volunteer with a steward, responsible for taking care of everyday responsibilities. That may sound like a luxury, but a Peace Corps volunteer just doesn't have time to take care of things like cleaning the house and fixing meals. Not only that, but the water had to be boiled and filtered, and all of the vegetables had to be washed in a special solution as a precaution against diseases our American digestive systems had no defenses for. My steward, Francis, did those things, letting me devote my time to developing my science curriculum. I also taught Francis how to make some foods we were more accustomed to — tacos, cheeseburgers, french fries, pizza. I trained Francis as one of Africa's first fast-food short-order cooks.

Of course, it wasn't Nigeria that was alien, it was us. For most of the village people, we were the first white people they'd seen. Children would come up to us, touch our skin, look at each other and laugh. We were used to a culture where blacks had been oppressed for so long, there was always a barrier that had to be negotiated before blacks and whites could be comfortable together. But here were Nigerian children walking right up to us, pulling on our hair and just laughing out loud, the most natural reaction in the world. We were the funniest things they'd ever seen, with this thin, scraggly hair and skin so pale you could see the veins.

I was teaching in Nigeria, but I was learning at the same time. I found myself growing more interested in intellectual pursuits, in political issues. I was living in a developing country, the kind of environment where ideas are always fermenting. I would sit in the village and drink palm wine with people who saw the world from a very different perspective from the one I'd brought from Southern California.

I tried hard to distance myself from that perspective — a *foreign* perspective, now. I didn't want to be the ugly American. I worked hard to be sensitive, aware of the culture's customs and taboos. I took pride in my ability to appreciate Nigerian culture. I was replacing the emptiness I'd felt in childhood, and even the somewhat artificial confidence I'd felt at Santa Barbara, with an emerging identity as a politically sensitive world citizen.

It's difficult to know sometimes, when you're dealing with a culture that's developed over millennia, what technological "benefits" of our society we should push on them. One volunteer in my group had been assigned to develop a farming cooperative among the tribes in the delta, people who for centuries had relied entirely on fishing. He was supposed to sell the tribes on the notion of growing date palm trees in this swampy region.

I agreed to go with him for a meeting he had arranged with one of the tribal chiefs. He picked me up in his fanboat, and we headed into the delta. By the time we'd gone just a few miles from Port Harcourt, we were in marshland fed by the ocean, an area so remote it was beyond anything you'll see in National Geographic. He knew his way around, picking the right tributaries and meandering through the desolate swamp.

We were in no man's land — well, no, that's not quite true. On the way to the village, we passed black market villages and bootleg traders' ships heading into Port Harcourt from the ocean. There were smuggler coves, where a person could pick up liquor, drugs, tobacco, anything. I guess you could say we were in no government land. And in fact the tribe we were visiting hadn't seen a government representative of any kind since 1952, 14 years earlier.

Teaching, Learning 35

When we arrived at the village, we were treated like kings. The chief greeted us and took us to his hut. We were very concerned about protocol. The people in the village knew of no other culture or other way of doing things, and we had to make sure we did things the right way and didn't insult anyone. We were constantly checking the cues from the people to make sure we did the right thing.

After we'd been sitting with the chief for a while, he raised his arm, and a boy came into the hut with a shovel and started digging into the dirt floor in the middle of the living room. After a bit of digging, there was a solid clunk, and the boy pulled out an old chest. The village chief opened this buried treasure and pulled out two Fanta orange sodas and some Nigerian beer. He opened the bottles and handed them to us. Apparently, the bottles had been buried for years in the chief's living room for a special event, and so naturally, we were honored and drank it. Then someone brought in some food — I don't know what it was, and I didn't want to know — and we washed it down with our aged Fanta orange. You don't want to offend anyone by asking, "What is this?" You just eat it and hope for the best.

The other volunteer began lobbying for the farm co-op idea, explaining to the village chief why palm trees should be planted to augment the village fishing income. It was a pretty basic economic idea, but it went counter to all their assumptions about how they should use their environment. We were trying to change centuries of history with tree seeds. They would have meetings and debate the issue, one side saying the village should continue as it always had, the other side saying they should listen to these new ideas.

We stayed in this village of 300 for three days, trying to push the date palms. No telephones, no electricity, we were completely out of touch with what we thought of as civilization. Even the smugglers village was miles away, and Port Harcourt was four or five hours by fanboat.

It was there, in fact, that I had my most frightening experience in Africa. My Peace Corps colleague, another man and I went hiking one night and got caught in a tropical shower. When I say "shower" in this region, I'm not talking about a drizzle: a wall of water was falling on us, sending us scurrying for cover. Suddenly the guy we were with fell to his knees and began gagging violently. He wore a dental plate, and his denture had shaken loose while he was running and lodged deep in his throat.

Here we were at least three hours away via jetboat in pitch blackness from a smugglers village with a shortwave radio. Even if we'd been there, it might be hours before someone would answer our call. We were hours away from medical help, but this guy might be 30 seconds away from choking to death. My colleague held him and I dropped my fingers down as far as I could into his throat. I pulled out the dental plate, and we heard his lungs fill with air. He gagged and choked for a few more minutes before coming out of it, and then all we could do was look at each other, we couldn't say a word. Growing up in America, where medical help was always as close as the phone and minutes away, it was incomprehensible to be in this life-and-death position where we were absolutely on our own. What if he had died? It would have been days before anyone would have known.

That was a sobering experience, but sobriety didn't characterize our adventures as much as absurdity did. One weekend, some of us tried to visit Fernando Po, an island to the south, off the coast of Cameroon. It's called Bioko now and belongs to Equatorial Guinea, but then it was a Spanish protectorate, and it was notorious as an island with no laws. It was supposedly a pirate haven full of gamblers and thieves and thugs. For four young adventurers, the lure was irresistible.

First, we had to get to Calabar, an infamous slave center. From there we could catch a boat for Fernando Po. We rode a lorry, an old truck where you just sit where you can, typically on top of the goats or the produce. As we were taking the ferry into Calabar, we saw a ship heading out of the harbor. It turned out that was the boat to Fernando Po — the twice-monthly boat, which we'd missed by 10 minutes.

We asked around and found out that there was another boat, and we bought tickets for it. For two days, we wandered through Calabar, this notorious slave trading center. Finally, the morning of our adventure arrived. We grabbed our tickets and headed down to the dock, where we were immediately struck by two things. First, there was an old rusted-out, black cast-iron tub; if it was really a boat, I think it must have been either the Monitor or the Merrimack. The other thing that caught our attention was that there were about 2,000 people on the shore waiting to board.

But we had tickets. We walked down to the shore proudly waving our tickets and found out that they sell a ticket to as many people as want one — like to all 2,000 people here. At that point, we went into our ugly American act, demanding to see the captain. Our plan was to convince him that we had important business on Fernando Po and that our tickets must be honored.

We were led onto this tiny rust tub and down to the captain's quarters. The stench belowdecks was unbelievable, and they led us to a fat, greasy, unshaven, smelly man lying down there, asleep, apparently hung over, flies buzzing all around him. The captain. We woke him up and discovered he spoke no English, and we didn't speak enough Spanish. Still half asleep, he just looked at us with a bewildered stare, then waved us off. They laughed us off the boat.

As soon as they opened the ship for boarding, it looked like the San Francisco 49ers on kickoff coverage, 2,000 people trying to cram their way onto the deck. Within five minutes it was jam-packed, and as soon as it was full, the 1,950 or so who didn't get on just picked up their stuff and walked away. It was a weekly ritual, and everybody but us had known what to expect.

Later that night, we were drinking beer in the hotel bar when we met an Italian pilot. He started buying us beers and telling us how he was a mercenary pilot for the Nigerian government — "I fly low over the delta, spotting smugglers," he said. We talked him into flying us to Fernando Po the next day. He asked for half of the money up front — about $100, as I recall — and half at the airport. We showed up at the airport the next day and of course there was no Italian pilot. Our last-ditch effort was to ask around for a smuggler to row us out in a canoe. One guy offered to take us in a hollowed-out canoe with about a 2 1/2-horsepower outboard motor — to an island 80 miles away. Good sense finally got the better of our adventurer's spirit, and we gave up our quest.

During 1966 and '67, the Nigerian civil war began to heat up between the Ibo in the eastern region, where I lived, and the rest of the nation. The dispute had begun centuries before over religious and tribal differences but had become an economic conflict by 1966. The Ibo were blamed for much of the unhappiness and strife in the rest of the nation.

Americans were told to avoid any potentially dangerous situations. One weekend, I was headed to Onitsha in a taxicab. That was the easiest way to travel from city to city — via taxi, an old Peugeot 404 station wagon. It was really more like pay-as-you-go car pooling: the cabs would congregate in a taxi park in the middle of town, and people would choose a taxi based on their destination. The taxi wouldn't leave until it was full. A typical ride cost seven shillings, about a dollar.

Everywhere we went there would be roadblocks. Nothing was structured, it was just guerrillas with guns. On this particular day, another Peace Corps volunteer, a young woman, got in the cab with me. She had just come in from the bush and had waited six months for an appointment to see the dentist in Onitsha, one of the few in the country. She was in no mood to be detained.

Now all Peace Corps personnel are issued identification cards, but nobody knew what they were for. It was something you got and when you reached your outpost you tossed it on a bookshelf somewhere and that's the last you ever thought about it. Most people didn't carry any identification at all. What good's a California driver's license in Nigeria?

So naturally, on this day our taxicab was stopped at a random roadblock, and the police demanded to see our Peace Corps IDs. Neither one of us had it along, so one policeman got in the cab with us and ordered the driver to take us to the station for questioning. I could see this was going to take forever, so I told the woman I'd distract the policeman and the driver when I got a chance so that she could grab her bag and head for the dentist.

The driver took all the locals to their various stops, but he wouldn't let us off at our downtown stop. Before going to the police station, though, he stopped for gas, and we set the Great Escape in motion. I went over and started asking the policeman and the driver all kinds of questions, and the woman grabbed her bags and ran. When the policeman and the driver realized what was going on, they went berserk, and I took that opportunity to grab my bag out of the back of the cab and try to make my escape. When the policeman stopped me, it was my turn to go berserk. I pointed out that I was in this country to help his people, not to be treated like this. As I grabbed my bag, the policeman clamped down on my arm. For a second, I was ready to give him a shove and take off running. Then I noticed that a mob of 200 to 300 people had gathered around us. I was the only non-Nigerian. I quickly calculated the odds and got back into the cab.

I was taken downtown to the police station and arrested as a spy. At this point, I was still taking everything pretty lightly.

Teaching, Learning

As each hour went by, my predicament got less and less funny.

I think these guys had watched one too many Peter Lorre movies. They put me in a chair in the middle of the room, and they'd walk slowly around the chair and interrogate me. "Who are you? Where do you teach? How do we know you're telling the truth?" One of them had a riding crop, and he'd bang it against my chair and on the table while he asked questions. Suddenly it dawned on me: these people could do anything they wanted. No one knew who I was or where I was. The only other person who knew I was in jail was the taxi driver, and he'd long since scurried back out into the middle of Nigeria in his Peugeot, never again to be seen by me or by anyone who knows me. Here I was, no money, no one phone call like in the movies — as far as I knew, there wasn't even a phone.

Finally one of the interrogators walked in and found a letter from my mother stashed in the bottom of my tote bag. The guy slapped the letter and walked around shouting, "Aha! Aha!" I didn't know whether that was good or bad until he held up the letter and said, "I see that you are telling the truth."

I was relieved, of course, but at the same time, I thought, "This is insane." This guy had pulled out a letter that may have been my letter or may have been somebody else's. On the letter is my name and my college in Port Harcourt. If this guy really suspected me as a spy, this was hardly the piece of ironclad evidence that was going to clear me. For four hours, nobody had gone through my bag, and I'd been giving them names of people in Onitsha who could identify me. All they had to do was find one of those people to vouch for me. But no, none of that mattered. But the letter — "Aha!" Thanks, Mom.

They opened the door and said, "Be careful — it's very dangerous for expatriates." Yeah, I noticed. I walked out with no idea where I was in this unfamiliar city. Finally I found my friend, one of my basketball pals, Ross Jennings, who had been waiting for me all day. He was with the St. Louis Hawks.

There were increasing signs that the civil war was about to explode in our faces. There was growing tension, and a strong anti-imperialist, anti-expatriate sentiment. To some extent, American Peace Corps volunteers were lumped together with the Europeans.

The Third World is a place of great contrast. Less than a mile down the road from my house was the magnificent 15-story

Presidential Hotel — air-conditioned, swimming pool, bar, theater. It had been built by the British and now catered to the businessmen drawn to Port Harcourt, which was a center of international trade. One hundred yards from the Presidential Hotel — I actually paced it off one day, almost exactly 100 yards — were people living in mud huts.

Some people appreciated the Peace Corps volunteers because they saw that we were in Nigeria to help others and that we didn't have a lot of money. We were living just like the people we were helping. On the other hand, there was a growing sentiment for independence from all outside interference. We rarely encountered any resistance in our local schools, but we would run into problems when we headed into the cities.

There were reports in newspapers of beatings, and increased violence, some of it against outsiders. I remember walking through the bush near my village one time and seeing a man with a nail driven into his skull. All over the country people were being ambushed and killed.

I was supposed to spend two full years in Nigeria, but as the political situation continued to deteriorate, we were left no choice. All Peace Corps volunteers were evacuated from Nigeria in early 1968.

The Nigerian experience was important to my development in several ways. For one thing, if any racial or ethnic insensitivity had survived my early years in San Bernardino, it was obliterated now. The experience also deepened my sense of what it means to be a minority, and to be a foreigner.

Ethnocentrism — the tendency to view the entire world through our own cultural lenses — is hard to escape when you're growing up in America. We learn from the time we start school that America is the best country in the world, and that's probably true, but unfortunately the underside of that message seems to be that everyone else's country, everyone else's culture is inferior. As a result, a lot of Americans grow up unable to see the world through any other lenses, to see other cultures as different but not necessarily inferior.

Experiencing the Third World, seeing the economic and cultural realities in Nigeria, absolutely "de-ethnocentrized" my perspective. Living among the Ibo made it clearer to me than any sociology or political science course ever could have that the middle-class white American way of looking at the world is just *one* way, not *the* way. It made me appreciate that trees can dance.

CHAPTER 5

THE WHOLE WORLD IS WATCHING

I wish I'd been able to talk to the guy who spit on me. I'm not sure it was a veteran, but I saw a lot of VFW caps in the crowd that was hassling us as we marched. But then I saw plenty of union pins, too, and I also saw young people who looked a lot like us. It seemed like everybody agreed we were scum for protesting the Vietnam War. That spit could have come from anyone.

But I always wished I could just sit down and have a conversation with one of those people who were so outraged by what we were doing, particularly the veterans. I wanted to explain that I had studied history and knew that the wars they had fought in Europe and the Pacific had been necessary. I wanted to make the case that Vietnam was not a war we needed to fight, that it had nothing to do with the survival of our homeland. I wanted to talk about losing my father in a war very much like this one. I wanted to tell these veterans I had pretty deep reasons for standing in that protest line, and that their spitting on me didn't address those reasons. Just ask me why I am holding this sign and I'll be glad to tell you, sir. But there was no chance to explain anything. It was chaos, people screaming and swearing at us.

I had returned from Nigeria a man without a plan again, and I found the re-entry to an American lifestyle surprisingly difficult. I'd become accustomed to life without television, radio and the other amenities of modern culture. Having a hot shower, taking a trip to the mall, talking on the telephone — all of this was as hard to readjust to as it had been to adjust to the deprivation of Africa.

And I had little idea what had been happening in the United States while I was away. We had the international edition of the *New York Times, Time,* and *Newsweek,* plus the local Nigerian papers. But just reading stories in the papers about student protests gave me little sense of the change that was taking place.

So I was a stranger in a strange land again. I had given some thought to graduate school, but I didn't want to rush into it. I actually wound up flipping hamburgers again for a while in a fast food stand in Newport Beach, still trying to map out my future.

Back in my Cal-Santa Barbara days, I had become friends with the dean of students there, Stephen Goodspeed. I had worked with Stephen quite a bit and decided I would enjoy that sort of career, working with students. Before I left for the Peace Corps, Stephen gave me the names of three schools he felt would best prepare me for a career in university administration. One of the schools on his list was Indiana University, so when my burger-flipping hiatus was done, I headed for the Midwest, leaving Newport Beach for Bloomington, Indiana.

I liked Bloomington from the moment I landed in the community. I enjoyed my graduate studies and made many friends. More to the point, I finally started to get my life in gear again after Africa. The world was changing, and my life was changing with it. The civil rights movement. The anti-war movement. The women's liberation movement. All of these movements were consuming my generation, and the IU campus was alive with demonstrations, protests, and the electricity of change. I began to embrace the various movements, and I felt illuminated. I read volumes of literature on the issues, and what I read made sense to me. These were causes that fit perfectly with my personality and my view of the world.

Over the years my sense of my place on the planet had evolved radically. When I was a kid in Catholic school, I was taught a view of the world that allowed for no ambiguity. But once I went away to college and learned that there were different ways of thinking, I realized I had two choices: blindly accept what I'd been told, or step back and ask, "What account of the world makes the most sense?" I chose the latter course.

The more I studied and developed my view of the world, the more I realized that it would be virtually impossible for me to believe that what I saw around me was created by some sort of spiritual being. In fact, I found it hard to accept that there was anything outside the immediate realities we confront from day to day. What that conclusion meant was that while many people grow up and live their lives with a feeling of security about a supreme being who takes care of eternity for them, I didn't have that luxury. All my reading and my reasoning and my experience led me to conclude that life must be lived, decisions must be made, based on the here and now.

I examine things in the here and now much more closely than others do, because that's all I have. So when I'm confronted with any sort of injustice, I have no patience with it, no sense that, "Well, in another life, God will reward those who are suffering now." I feel an emotional upheaval, and I react immediately, uncompromisingly.

I read the continental philosophers from Hegel to Marx to Lenin to Herbert Marcuse, and I found a common rubric of dialectical materialism in those works that matched my own philosophy: here is how the world proceeds, in real physical terms, not in some abstract set of rules we can memorize in a catechism. Given that philosophy, it seemed only natural to get involved with the movements that were trying to correct what was wrong with the world.

Enormous changes in my personal life were close at hand, too. I met Anna Judkins at a party in Bloomington in 1968, and we dated for a year and a half before being married in 1969. My first child, Becky, was born a year later. Suddenly, I had responsibilities far beyond my own life, and I was surprised how enthusiastically I accepted them. From the minute Becky was born, I was ecstatic about being a dad. From changing diapers at the start to helping with homework a few years later, I wanted to share in everything, I wanted to be involved with this amazing new life. I'd had my own father ripped away from me so violently, but now I had a chance to *be* a father, to have someone need me that way.

Marriage and parenthood accelerated my acceptance of a role in the many political movements of the day as well, because Anna is black. As a white man married to a black woman, I had my first direct taste of racism. Growing up in California, I had seen racism, but I'd also seen races living together and getting along. I had never been able to understand why one person could hate another just because of racial or cultural differences. It was clear to me early on who the good guys and the bad guys were in the fight for racial justice.

But now the issue wasn't just some abstraction. It affected my wife, my daughter. It had become a personal issue. Over the years, I've had to face racism and I've had to see my children face it more times than I care to remember. It's ugly, insensitive, irrational. Mostly, it just hurts, and the anger that it breeds is completely justifiable.

I didn't marry Anna to prove a point or to do my bit toward solving racial injustice. In fact, an interracial marriage creates unbelievable problems. Nobody in his right mind would invite that sort of trouble without feeling a strong personal commitment. But within that relationship, I became more aware than ever before that there's a world where non-whites live that is completely apart from anything that the white community can fathom, and that's as true today as it was 50 years ago.

Tied to that, I think non-whites are far more attuned than Caucasians to the cues that suggest someone is racially insensitive. And within my marriage, I developed some of the same sort of intuition. The levels of complexity and sophistication in my understanding of the racial situation in this country became much clearer to me.

And so I became more and more involved in civil rights demonstrations, always walking in protest lines, cheering speakers, providing support any way I could. We backed the movement, pushing for desegregation and voting rights, crying out against the likes of George Wallace in Alabama and Orval Faubus in Arkansas, governors who seemed to feel a responsibility only to the white people of their states. And I made the decision not just to battle racism in the rest of the world, but to bring the message home. In my dealings with other whites, I made a personal commitment to educating others about race relations. That sometimes made life a little more difficult — and always a little more interesting. I'm sure there were people who didn't want to be around me because of it. I tried not to be the big bad thought policeman, but when I saw racism, I was determined to say something about it.

After Becky was born, I became even more militant about it, more committed to straightening out racial insensitivity wherever I encountered it. The guy who's telling that racist joke, who's making that narrow-minded remark — that guy may come in contact with my daughter someday, and I don't want her to be a veteran of that kind of bigotry.

I had a personal stake in the antiwar movement, as well. But beyond having seen and lived through what my father's death had done to my family, I began to educate myself about the role of the American government throughout the world. I discovered it wasn't all that we had been told in school, starting with Columbus' "discovery" of America. How can you discover a land someone else is already living in? The whole language of history was ethnocentric, based on the assumption that these backward natives should welcome the progress brought them by the advanced Europeans. If you look at it a little more objectively, Columbus wasn't a great explorer, he was a hired economic agent of Spain. He was an imperialist. And he set an unfortunate tone for this country's future.

I studied the role of the U.S. government in Chile in the 1960s and '70s and how the American government had tried to dominate Latin America and South America. Our government had suppressed nationalistic feelings in these countries in order to keep them under economic control. It was the old ethnocentric, imperialist impulse again — what's good for us is good for everybody.

I was never ashamed to be an American, but I was ashamed of some things America was doing, and I felt obliged to express my feelings. So I got involved in more demonstrations and expressions of political discontent. That didn't mean I wasn't a loyal American. "America: Love it or leave it" was a favorite battle cry of those who wanted the protesters to shut up. Well, I've always loved this country, and I've never wanted to leave it. America has been a world leader in so many positive ways, and its achievements are unmatched in history. Other countries look to us as a model in the quest for democratic rights. It's precisely *because* of what America is and what it stands for that many of us have tried to push our government to correct what seem like obvious mistakes in policy. I was a member of several organizations dedicated to that purpose, and I contributed my viewpoints to the campus underground newspaper on occasion.

The revelations of the government itself since Vietnam vindicate almost all of what the antiwar movement was about. At the time, the government denied everything we said; today, the antiwar movement seems to have been "right on." I think our leaders were genuine in their intentions, but the Vietnam War was a mistake, an example of disastrously ill-informed decision making. Our government made some terrible mistakes, and I feel justified in having been part of a movement that helped spawn a more accountable foreign policy.

The war itself, of course, was hideous. When I was in Africa, I corresponded with friends in Vietnam and ones who had been there. The stories were horrible. My friends, people I'd grown up with — people like me — had been asked to do some atrocious things and had atrocious things done to them. And some of my friends never made it home. It was a dark chapter in American history.

The war was there all the time, it filtered into every part of your life. Watching this horrible war on television for one night made you want to do something about it. But seeing it night after night had almost a numbing effect. Every night, we would hear the body count, the number of soldiers killed that day. After hearing it day after day after day, the numbers almost lost their meaning — your mind just wouldn't let you accept the meaning any more. And always in the back of your mind was the possibility that you'd be next — that you'd be drafted and have to face the horror of it firsthand.

For some of my friends in the military, the war became a wedge between us. They were in the military and were being sent to Vietnam and had to buy into the war effort to stay alive. They didn't have the luxury to think about the morality and the politics of it. Their primary obligation was to stay alive. Again, remember we're talking about a group of people born right after World War II, who had grown up wrapped in the security blanket of the American Dream. There was no place in that dream to doubt our country's leaders.

The protests were frightening affairs. During the demonstration at Indiana University, I was spit on more than once, but that was nothing. The police and the National Guard were often standing by, guns at the ready, and there was a feeling of imminent danger and trouble. A demonstration really tested your inner strength. Even when there was no physical assault, you were met by a storm of ridicule and hatred, the objects of animosity and intolerance. The worst part was realizing that even within my generation, among people who had grown up in a similar background to mine, the majority didn't agree with

The Whole World is Watching   47

what I was doing. It didn't take long to realize that if I really didn't believe in the cause, if this wasn't really what I stood for, then I should get out. All along, I felt we were thinking each issue through to its correct conclusion and standing up for that conclusion. Reflecting back on it today, I still feel that way. We were sometimes naive, there's no question about that, but at bottom we were right.

Naive — I guess when a lot of people think back to that era, all they remember are the songs and the chants and the slogans. I was never much for chants. Chanting at a protest always seemed like shouting "Block that kick!" at the football game. This was more serious than that. When I was asked to speak or make a presentation, I would stand up and give my speech and be done with it. No chants or songs. Then again, come to think of it, I've never been a big one for chants at ball games, either.

I can't say the movement was filled by nothing but wonderful philosophers — there were a lot of jerks, just like in the rest of the population. But there were genuine people, too, telling genuine truths about what was going on. Who was I going to listen to instead, Richard Nixon, telling me that everything was terrific? The movement helped shape a lot of us, shape us for the better. And the era also produced some genuine heroes, people who are still making a difference today, long after their deaths.

The assassinations that year were incredible, Martin Luther King Jr. and Bobby Kennedy. Those senseless deaths took me back to 1965, when Malcolm X was assassinated. I'd read his autobiography and thought it was the best possible document of the Civil Rights movement. From the moment Malcolm was shot, I was convinced that either the American government or the Nation of Islam had a hand in his death.

A friend I worked with in grad school who was from the South came back from spring break and said he was on a bus in Atlanta when someone got on and shouted to everyone, "Hey, they just shot Martin Luther Coon!" As if the assassination wasn't devastating enough, there were still people who not only had attitudes like that, but were proud of those attitudes, would shout them out on a crowded bus.

I was in Chicago shortly after Dr. King's death, when the National Guard took over the streets of the city. Anna was from the South Side of Chicago, so I had an opportunity to spend time inside an urban black culture that wasn't filtered through a need to survive in white society. There are two cultures, the unguarded, natural culture and the one exhibited to the white power structure. My being married to Anna gave me an "in" to the more genuine culture, and I had a sense of the blacks' resentment over the armed soldiers patrolling the streets on the South Side. The tension was so acute, I was always ready to duck in somewhere if trouble started in the streets.

A couple of months later, Bobby Kennedy made an appearance in Bloomington. I wasn't necessarily a Democrat in '68, but Bobby Kennedy stood for a lot of the right things and I wanted to help out. I was part of the group that had helped arrange the Kennedy appearance, and I got to meet him at the hotel. A few days after I'd shaken his hand, Bobby Kennedy was dead.

I wasn't in Chicago for the Democratic National Convention that summer, but I remember watching on television, when Hubert Humphrey was given his sham nomination while Mayor Daley's cops were cracking heads in the streets. "The whole world is watching," was the protestors' chant, and that was the theme for that whole era. The world can't have much liked what it saw.

I had a life away from the protest marches, too, of course. I was a full-time graduate student with a wife and a baby daughter, and I couldn't let my responsibilities to the world get in the way of my responsibilities at home. In between marching and going to classes, I brought in a little money with some part-time jobs, including a position educating public school teachers in Louisville one day per week. Then a group of us started a family child care cooperative, the Big Monster Family House. We leased a house and built a day care center for our children, everybody working shifts feeding the kids, clothing them, changing diapers, taking them on field trips. It was part of the political spirit of the time, a way of sharing our lives and our responsibilities and of giving the children a broader outlook than if their parents were the only adults they knew.

One regular volunteer at the Big Monster Family House was a Vietnam veteran named Bill Harris. I had met Bill when we both had small parts as slave ship sailors in a production of *In White America* at the Black Theater Workshop in Bloomington. Bill and I became good friends and taught a summer school course together in educational issues.

About a year after Bill left Indiana for California, Anna and I visited him and his wife Emily in Oakland. After one visit, while we were living in Pittsburgh, we saw Bill's picture on a network news report on the Patty Hearst kidnapping. Our old friend, we suddenly realized, was one of the founders of the Symbionese Liberation Army. Because I had stayed in touch with Bill, the FBI started taking an interest in my activities. A mailman who had us on his route confided to me at one point that our mail was being opened daily. An agent was parked in front of my mother's house for several months, as well, because I'd given Bill her address in case I moved. Apparently they tapped my phone as well, because everyone else I was in touch with during that period had visits from the Bureau. The FBI eventually caught up with Bill and he served time in a California prison.

We had known Bill as an antiwar activist, but we were unprepared for this kind of scrutiny. Whatever people might think about Bill's political activities, he was one of the most popular adults at Big Monster. Just ask my daughter Becky. The co-op was enormously rewarding for both the adults and the children, and it was also a way to save some money on baby-sitting. We were living on pennies, getting by from day to day. There weren't a lot of pleasure trips, or even free moments.

My political activism eventually altered the course of my academic career, and at the same time it gave me a greater incentive to work hard at my studies. I changed my major from educational administration to philosophy of education, with a minor in philosophy. I studied social and political philosophy and how the institution of formal education fit within certain social philosophies. I also took courses in international education. My central focus was to understand the evolution of education within an overall social order. Upon what ideas and principles is education based? My doctoral dissertation was a Marxist perspective on the evolution of the American education system. I surprised myself with the vigor of my intellectual pursuits, and I became a high achiever academically.

But as serious as I was about academics, and about politics, and about my family, there was still time for a little fun and games. Volleyball remained a sort of "secret passion." Athletics wasn't supposed to be a priority for anyone involved with the political movement in the late 1960s and early '70s, but I clung fast to sports, both as a fan and as a participant.

It was a great time to be a fan at Indiana, too. My first week on campus in 1967, I was studying in the library when I heard the crowd cheering from the football stadium, where the Hoosiers were rallying for a season-opening victory. At that point, I knew nothing about Big Ten football. I'd heard of some of the big rivalries, like Ohio State-Michigan, but I had no appreciation of the conference-wide tradition.

So my first Saturday there, Indiana pulled off what turned out to be the first in a long string of last-second football victories. The Hoosiers won the next week, as well, and pretty soon everybody was getting fired up over IU football. That was another thing I didn't realize: that at a basketball school like Indiana, enthusiasm for the football program was something out of the ordinary.

I started going to the football games later in the season and got to watch the best football team in Indiana history, the school's only Big Ten champion in the last 50 years. Harry Gonso was the quarterback, John Isenbarger played halfback, and Jade Butcher was a wide receiver. Coincidentally, a defensive back on that team, Mike Deal, has since come to Illinois as an assistant football coach, and he and I are neighbors in Champaign. We never knew each other during our time together at IU, but we've had some good times reminiscing about that championship season. Indiana went to the Rose Bowl and lost to USC and O.J. Simpson, 14-3.

I was at Indiana during the Mark Spitz years, too, under legendary swimming coach Doc Counsilman. The swimming world knew all about the Indiana swimming program long before Spitz got there, but by the time he came back from Munich with his seven Olympic gold medals in 1972, the rest of the world had gotten the message, too.

And a couple of years after I came to IU, Lou Watson stepped down as head basketball coach and was replaced by a young rabble-rouser from Army, with jet-black hair and plaid sports coats. We used to watch the new guy, Bob Knight, and his teams in the old IU Fieldhouse. It wasn't long before this young coach was putting great teams on the floor. I was learning what Big Ten sports was all about, quite a switch from the laid-back athletic atmosphere in Southern California.

Of course, there'd never been anything laid-back about my participation in sports, but at Indiana I cranked my volleyball game up another notch. There was a club team run by Jerry Yaegely, better known as Indiana's soccer coach. We played in the Midwest Intercollegiate Volleyball Association, varsity and club teams playing in the same league.

I didn't realize it at the time, but the Midwest had become a volleyball hotbed by the '70s. Don Shondell was coaching at Ball State, producing young coaches like Mick Haley, Jim Stone, and Arnie Ball. Doug Beal and Terry Liskeyvich were at Ohio State, along with Suguru Furuichi, a Japanese national coach. Jim Coleman, who was coaching at George Williams College, is now the technical director for the U.S. men's and women's teams. Jerry Angle, the Northwestern coach, was playing and coaching at the time. Russ Rose, now at Penn State, was playing in the MIVA (Midwest Intercollegiate Volleyball Association). Stu McDole, now an American Volleyball Coaches Association board member, played on our team.

If I'd known how many volleyball careers were waiting for these MIVA guys, maybe I'd have had a little better sense of what my own future held.

Iron City Sojourn

I began my dissertation in 1971, and I could hardly have chosen a worse time. In the early '70s, higher education began to feel the economic crunch for the first time. Up to that time, the message in graduate school had been simple: get a Ph.D., get a job. That was the way it worked when I started in 1967, but now the rules had changed. The year-end national convention for my field of study, the conference at which students had traditionally been recruited by colleges, had turned into a place where desperate students went begging. I remember having a drink with Phil Smith, my department chairman, during the convention, and he spent the time apologizing for the collapse of the job market. "Sorry," he told me, "there's nothing I can do. There are no jobs."

Dave Clark, the dean of the School of Education at Indiana, took a personal interest in one graduate student every year, making every effort to help that student find the right job. With the contacts he had and the prestige his recommendation carried, Dean Clark had never failed to find a good job for his "adopted" grad student, and I was the one he chose from my class. He wrote 52 letters on my behalf to academic colleagues across the nation, many of them personal friends. No dice. The job market had dried up so badly, even Dean Clark's influence couldn't help.

I applied for every teaching job even remotely related to my field and finally was hired as an assistant professor at Chatham College in Pittsburgh, a women's liberal arts school of 650 students. My specialties at Indiana had been philosophy and philosophy of education, but Chatham hired me to teach secondary school education. I would be teaching methods classes, the most basic introductory education courses. In fact, it was my Peace Corps training as an educator that got me the job, not my Ph.D.

Chatham was the only school interested in me so I took the job, and we moved to Pittsburgh in 1972. I wasn't prepared to like Pittsburgh, but I fell in love with the city and its people. I've always been fascinated with change, and I've never had trouble adjusting to new towns and new environments. Pittsburgh is a good, honest working-class town. The people there spot phonies pretty quickly. The ethnic variety in the city and in the city's food made it a little bit like being back home. On the other hand, the architecture and the history were revelations for someone from the West Coast. The city's rich history was exciting to learn about and to experience.

We lived in several parts of the city while we were in Pittsburgh, finally getting particularly involved in the Mexican War Streets area, a part of the city about a half-mile from Three Rivers Stadium that was being restored and rebuilt. We lived there for four years in two different homes, which we'd spend our weekends rebuilding. I was recently in Pittsburgh and drove by the old neighborhood. I had been gone for more than 15 years, but as I walked down the street, I heard someone yell, "Hey, Mike, what are you doing here?" So many people had stayed in the neighborhood, and they were still fixing up their houses. I felt right at home, just as I had when we lived in Pittsburgh.

Chatham, on the other hand, was a job I didn't enjoy, with people that I couldn't relate to. The campus is the former enclave of Andrew Mellon, the Pittsburgh steel baron. The student union, in fact, is the former Mellon mansion. The campus is as beautiful as you might guess, given its history, and as insulated from the blue-collar city. You've probably also gotten an idea of what social stratum the students came from.

Actually, I didn't have any problem with my upper-class students. In fact, throughout my two years, I got consistently high teaching evaluations. It was some of the faculty members, who also seemed to consider themselves part of the elite, that I didn't see eye-to-eye with. I didn't have much in common with my fellow faculty members or with the administrators.

Needless to say, my "radical" views were unpopular at Chatham. So, I quickly learned, was my mixed marriage. The first time my wife and I attended a school function, the president's reception for faculty, you could see the alarm and shock on the faces of other professors. It seemed more than a little ironic to have to endure insults and small-minded gossip at a "liberal arts" college.

It was made clear to me after my second year at Chatham that I was not welcome to return for a third. I don't know if I'd actually have been fired if I refused to resign, but it didn't matter. The arched-eyebrow posture of the administration had become a bore, and I gladly gave them the resignation they wanted.

Adding to the difficulty of my years at Chatham was my ongoing work on my dissertation. I would teach during the day, then head for the University of Pittsburgh library at night, stealing a few hours in between to spend with my family. We had one car, and Anna and I had to juggle our schedules constantly. I finished the dissertation in 1973, late in my first year in Pittsburgh, and Indiana conferred my Ph.D. on me in 1974.

I was still a political activist. In Pittsburgh, I learned about the steelworkers' movement and began attending meetings and handing out leaflets at the mills, trying to drum up support for the union. I met several autoworkers and steelworkers and learned about the old days in the plants. One day, the great folk singer, Pete Seeger showed up with his banjo and played for about 50 people at a meeting.

I became close friends with Dave Montgomery, who was a leading professor of labor history at the University of Pittsburgh. Besides our shared interest in the labor movement, Dave and his wife, Marty, were also partners in an interracial marriage, so we shared some defining experiences on that front, too. Dave is still one of the most prominent figures in the labor history field.

After leaving Chatham, I hit some rocky times. I worked as a substitute teacher in the Pittsburgh public schools for a while. That was quite a jolt back to real life after the cultural cocoon of Chatham. So was having to go on unemployment for six months. At one point, I took the firefighter's exam for the city of Pittsburgh. I'd have taken the job, too, had I qualified. Meanwhile, the gas crisis had hit; when we could afford to gas up the car, we had to wait in block-long lines to do it.

Finally, in 1975, I was hired as a permanent substitute at Peabody High School, teaching ninth-grade social science. Peabody was in a very rough neighborhood in the inner city, and it had more than its share of trouble. In my second week there, a girl in my class was arrested for murder. I had regular visits from the police, narcotics agents, and probation officers. Peabody was an armed camp. Still, I really prized my time there. I enjoyed the challenge, and I actually found it more intellectually stimulating than Chatham had been. Here, people were dealing with real-life issues.

A year later, I got a job as a full-time social studies teacher at Mt. Lebanon High School in the south suburbs. This was a country club atmosphere compared with Peabody. During my two-year tenure there, my career would take an improbable turn.

When a volleyball player moves to a new community, it usually doesn't take long to get in touch with the local V-ball network. When I moved to Pittsburgh, I soon learned that the best game in town was at the Allegheny YMCA on the north side. I started haunting the YMCA on Wednesday nights for three hours of volleyball and a beer at a local pub afterward. The Wednesday night ritual had been a part of Pittsburgh volleyball for years; I'm guessing Allegheny is probably still the place to play.

There was a core group of 12 to 15 people for the Wednesday night Allegheny YMCA league, plus a rotating group of 20 or 30 — people blowing in and out of town, people who didn't make it every week. On Wednesday nights, a group of 30 to 40 people would find its way to the Y to play volleyball and talk volleyball. I was about 30 — the kid on the beach was history, but I was still fairly athletic.

On the beach, you do whatever you have to do — you pass, you set, you hit, you serve, you dig, you do everything. In college, I had been an outside hitter — I could jump well, I could hit the ball hard, and I had a really good feel for anticipating the block. By the time I moved to Pittsburgh, my jumping ability had begun to diminish, and I became a setter. That's where I spent my last few years as a player. It was a fun trip through the game: I learned the passing and digging and outside hitting game, and then as I matured — well, aged, anyway; I'm not sure how much I matured — I became a setter.

The orchestrator of the Wednesday night league was Bruno Krsul, a guy who had to be in his late 40s, early 50s. Years before, he had played for the old St. Joe Lead team out of western Pennsylvania. Bruno was the guy — it was his game, his ball, and the action didn't really start until Bruno unlocked the gym. One Wednesday night in late 1975, Bruno pulled me aside. "You know, they're looking for a coach over at Pitt," he said.

Bruno had been asked to coach the University of Pittsburgh team, but had to turn it down due to work commitments. Then he'd looked around the group of Wednesday night players and thought of me. At first, I said I wasn't interested, but a few weeks later, Bruno cornered me again. Pitt was still looking. I promised Bruno I'd at least check out the job.

So check it out I did, and the first surprise was that we were talking about a women's team. I didn't even know there *was* a women's team. In fact, despite my interest in the women's movement, I wasn't in touch with the women's sports movement at all. I met with Sandy Bullman, Pitt's women's athletic director, and she outlined the job. That was the second surprise: it was a part-time job paying $2,500 a year. Still, the notion was intriguing, and I agreed to give it a shot: my first collegiate coaching job.

Except that I wasn't really thinking of it as the "first," because that would mean I had some grand plan to make volleyball coaching my career. My primary reason for taking the job was extra income for my young family. It was still hard hooking up with any kind of a job in the early to mid-70s. If I could convert my volleyball experience into a few extra bucks, all the better. I was curious about coaching the women's game, that's true, but at the same time, if something else had popped up that was equally interesting and offered more income, I wouldn't have stayed in coaching for long. In fact, forget "equally interesting" — it could have been $3,000 painting signs part time. I wasn't thinking, "Let me calculate exactly how a profession is going to be carved out here, and how someday I'm going to be a nationally respected coach." It was a part-time job that would bring in some extra money. As far as I was concerned, it was always going to be part time.

I'd been a player-coach for several U.S. Volleyball Association teams when I was at Indiana, but I was totally unprepared for the coaching experience. I had never coached professionally, certainly had never coached a female. In fact, I had never *seen* a women's college volleyball match — there hadn't been that many played at that point.

I held formal tryouts to start, and my first decision was to cut the returning setter from the 1975 team. I may not have known anything about women's athletics, but my volleyball experience told me that we weren't going to have a successful team centering our offense around a 4-foot-11 setter with bad hands. Naturally, waves of protest followed from parents, administrators, players, and boosters. College coaching Lesson 1: Learn how to handle public relations.

A few days later, I got the team together for our first practice session in Fitzgerald Fieldhouse. The 60-year-old Fieldhouse was home to the Pitt basketball team. The women's athletic office was at the top of Fitzgerald, as far from the rest of civilization as possible. That's "office," singular, with one secretary for all the women's coaches. I would climb the three flights of stairs to the women's athletic office and pick up my mail and messages. Then, since I had no office of my own, I would walk back out of the lobby into this cavernous arena and sit on the concrete and steel stairway — sort of like a fire escape. That's where I would go through my mail, answer my letters. If I had anything for the secretary to type, I'd take it back in, and she'd get to it when she could, depending on how much work the other coaches had for her.

So the 1976 Pittsburgh women's volleyball team met at the Fieldhouse for its first practice in early August. Reservation form in hand for the gym time, I arrived to find a basketball summer camp in progress. I found the Pitt basketball coach, Tim Grgurich, who later became Jerry Tarkanian's top assistant at UNLV, and showed him my reservation form.

"Gosh, I don't know what to tell you," Tim said, "but I've got kids who paid 150 bucks to be here, and we're going to have our basketball camp. I don't know who did this to you, but it's not my problem." He was as diplomatic as he could be, but he made it clear that my volleyball team wasn't ever going to come in and kick out his basketball camp. College coaching Lesson 2: Know your place.

I learned very quickly that the only way for a coach of a nonrevenue sport to avoid these "scheduling errors" was to get to know the person responsible for scheduling facilities and do whatever was necessary to get on that person's good side. In the meantime, our first "practice" was held on the lawn outside the Fieldhouse. I used the time to get to know the players. I sat down with my team and got right down to the basics: "How good are we?" I asked them "I've never seen you or any of your opponents — *our* opponents — play. What can I expect?" The last two questions I asked them were the most important: "Where did we finish last year? And how well can we do this year?"

The team set a goal to finish 12th in the region, matching its finish from the previous year. I challenged them, wondering aloud why we couldn't set a goal to finish fourth instead of 12th. I guess no one wanted to get on the new coach's bad side, so our team goal became to finish fourth in the region. And then we went out and matched our goal, going 27-5 and finishing fourth in the region.

The more I coached, the more I liked coaching. But college coaching Lesson 3 was that I didn't know how to coach, not women's volleyball anyway. My first day of practice, I showed up in my football coaching shorts with my whistle and clipboard, Woody Hayes Jr. Most of the coaches I'd seen were football and basketball coaches. I thought coaching was 75 percent inspirational speeches, 25 percent inspirational swearing. One thing I knew: I was supposed to live and die by victories and defeats.

That first year, I was an emotional basket case, every match. A Pitt victory put me on top of the world, though I rarely had any idea why we'd won. A loss sent me to — is there a level lower than basket case? All the while, I couldn't understand my female athletes' response to winning and losing. We'd lose a match and I would be close to hara-kiri, absolutely devastated. This was worse than torture and death. But the women just didn't get it — they thought life went on in spite of a loss. They seemed to think this was a *game*, for crying out loud. I remember getting on the team bus at the University of Delaware. We had just lost in the semifinals of a tournament, and I was absolutely destroyed. I turned around and the players were singing Girl Scout songs and doing all kinds of crazy stunts, happy as could be. I was stunned. It sent me into an even deeper depression.

We all had a lot to learn, and obviously I had as much to learn as any of my players. It took me a while to realize that, just as I had no role model for coaching women athletes, they had no role models to show them how to *be* female athletes. If a football player signed to play at Pitt, he would be immersed in the tradition of Pittsburgh football, he'd know about Mike Ditka and Tony Dorsett. The young football player would have an instant understanding of tradition and how to act as an athlete.

A female student-athlete in 1976 had no idea of how to act. She knew she wasn't there to be Mike Ditka, but there was no training, no background, no cultural model for what she was trying to do. There was no background for my situation either. A competitive male coach leading a group of Girl Scout singers — how was I supposed to react to that?

I had no idea how to treat female athletes. I would say things in practice that I had heard in my playing days and would find out two days later that I had offended half the team. What I thought of as constructive criticism would just deflate people. Boys grew up with that kind of coaching, and they knew the "code," but to the women of that era, it was brand new, aggressive and obnoxious. I had to learn the difference.

For their part, the players had to learn how to confront me with their objections. Once they realized that I was as willing to learn as they were, the players were tremendously patient with me. They learned to come and tell me when I'd crossed the line between coach and tyrant, to explain their objections to what I'd done, to ask questions about what I'd been trying to get across. They wanted to learn the sport, and I wanted to learn how to teach them the sport.

Meanwhile, we had to deal with logistical problems that women and coaches hadn't had to deal with before. Nowadays, we don't have to sit down as a team and decide what to wear when we are lifting weights next to the football players, but that was an issue then — "Well, how do we dress?" I wanted my athletes to take advantage of the weight machines in the training room, which raised a question no one had thought of yet. If you go to a health club or the Y, you're familiar with the abductor-adductor machines, where you spread your legs against resistance, then swing them together again. Well, in 1993 men and women use that machine in the same room all the time, and no one thinks anything of it. But in 1976, when a football player was much more inclined to think of a woman as a sex object than as a fellow athlete, some women were uncomfortable using the abs-ads machine with a bunch of guys gathered around leering.

This was no joke, these were legitimate questions. Do the females avoid certain exercises when there are men around, or should they not worry about that, should they just say, "Forget it — we're athletes too"? These questions were being asked for the first time, and they needed answers, and I was the one being asked, daily. "What do we wear on road trips?" Sometimes I wanted to say, "Call your mom; I don't know what you wear." But it was a fair question: without a tradition to lean on, without a precedent to refer to, what *do* varsity athletes wear on the bus, and the next question is what do they wear on the court? Tight-fitting outfits like the gymnasts', or loose-fitting uniforms? All these questions were brand new, and as trivial as they might seem now, they were serious concerns to these young women. Some players were concerned about being considered unfeminine because they were athletes. Some went so far as wearing ribbons and makeup during matches.

And as if all these complications weren't enough, some nights we'd actually play a match. I was still teaching at Mt. Lebanon, so on game nights I'd finish teaching my last class of the day, grab my grade books and homework assignments and race to my car. After battling Pittsburgh traffic to get to the gym, I'd duck into a public rest room to change clothes— remember, no coaches' offices or dressing rooms— and get to work. There were no managers, no maintenance people to help, and my assistant coach taught at a high school farther away than mine, so he wasn't there yet. The players were still in class, so there was no one to help. I did everything.

First, clean up the trash, sweep and damp mop the floor, pick up after whatever the gym's last recreational activity had been. Literally everything necessary to transform a facility that had been left in a shambles into a match site, the head coach had to do it. Next, set up the nets, roll out the bleachers, track down some chairs for team benches, plug in the public address system, get the little tape player for the national anthem — the kind you have to hold up right next to the microphone. Then, if I hadn't already made arrangements for concessions, I'd have to find someone to make sandwiches and popcorn and get someone to hand out programs to the 100 or so people who would show up. Of course, I'd already typed up and copied the programs at school, after calling the other team for roster information. I had to arrange for referees, arrange to get checks cut for the referees and have the checks in my pocket—it was part of my game attire. There was no such thing as event management. The coach did everything, and still does in some places.

I designed our uniforms, I carried the equipment in the trunk of my car, I had to make sure the game balls were pumped up. And then, after two or more hours of work to get the gym ready for the match, after no dinner, after being a superman maniac, then I'd start to get some company. The assistant coach would show up, and the players, and some people who helped out, and then they would all be maniacs. I'd head into our pregame meeting totally disheveled and exhausted, maybe with a migraine.

And then it would be, "Oh, wow, who do we play tonight? Is everybody here? And what are we going to do about one of the uniforms — it got ruined when we bleached it." So I'd be trying to figure out how to get another uniform, because we play in 45 minutes. And then I had to make sure everyone had their shoes. There were no extra shoes, of course — there was one pair of shoes that the players had to buy themselves. Finally, by the time we were ready to go, and the players were on the floor and warming up, I was so ragged I could hardly have coached the cap off a bottle of Iron City beer. And now it's show time — I'm supposed to start the game and be a coaching mastermind.

Inevitably the match starts with, "And now, our national anthem . . . click-click-click." I'd have to rush over, fix the cassette deck or show somebody, "Don't push that button, push this button." It was like a junior high assembly. And then the tape would be past the anthem into the warm-up tape, and one of those wild James Brown grunts would go out across the PA at about 90 decibels. Sometimes I'd have to pull someone out of the stands to sing the anthem. Then finally we'd get through the warm-ups, and the lineups would be announced over this sound system that sounded like an elevated train. And then the match would be played, *if* the referees had shown up.

It was hectic, it was insane, and, obviously, I loved it. I had taken a step into a very alien world, and we had some success, and I discovered I enjoyed coaching. I think I got a raise to $3,000 for my second season at Pitt. Still, as far as I was concerned, I was an academic first, an educator. I had my Ph.D. in history and philosophy of education, and I had secondary school certification in social studies. For all I knew, I was going to be a high school teacher all my life, and that was fine with me. Coaching volleyball was more of a curiosity.

The quick success of the program at Pittsburgh helped the volleyball team earn a little more respect within the athletic department. We upgraded our uniforms. We got shoes after a year or so. Year by year, things got better. I was a mad fundraiser, and at the same time, I wanted to put Pittsburgh volleyball in the public eye. I started a junior program, the Three Rivers Volleyball Club. We hosted international teams with the junior program and pushed volleyball to the state of Pennsylvania, getting an awful lot of people involved. Between our activities and those of people like Dr. Tom Tait, the Penn State men's and women's coach, we helped to establish volleyball in the Keystone State. And we didn't know it at the time, but we had become a significant force in the evolution of volleyball in the East.

Pittsburgh became the region's elite collegiate program. My first and second seasons, we finished fourth in the region. In my third and fourth seasons, we won the regional and advanced to the national championships, finishing in a tie for ninth in the nation both years. Pitt was widely considered to be the first team from the East to go out and play respectably against a West Coast team, to make it look like real volleyball.

And with the success, volleyball got to be kind of an exciting deal on campus. By the time we moved some of our matches across from the intramural facility to the Fitzgerald Fieldhouse, we were drawing crowds of up to 3,000 for playoff matches. Pittsburgh was a great sports town in the '70s: Tony Dorsett leading Pitt's football team to the national championship, the Steelers winning four Super Bowls, the Pirates winning a World Series. We may not have had the best-known team in Pittsburgh, but we were a small part of the city's golden age of sports.

I had begun to figure out this coaching game, too, and to develop a style that worked for me and for my athletes. My personality has always functioned better with intuition and creative expression than with a lock step agenda. I would rather look at the big picture and put together a scheme rather than plodding along, Point A to Point B, Point B to Point C. If someone tells me, "Here's the curriculum, teach it," I can do it, but I'm not at my best, and I become impatient with the restrictions. I'm at my best when I'm presented with a problem and given the leeway to solve it.

If you watch me in the gym even today, within minutes of starting a drill, I am working variations into it to make it more interesting. That's what I like most about working with elite athletes. Most athletes need the steady repetition: do it this way, over and over and over. I can do that, but I'm like a horse chafing at the bit. When I work with elite athletes, people at the cutting edge, they've already established a fundamental base, and I can work past the fundamentals to solve individual problems in new and innovative ways.

I started to notice something else about coaching female athletes. The instinct for racial insensitivity I'd been developing over the years translated to this arena as well. John Lennon sang about woman being the "nigger of the world," and that was exactly what I found in athletics. Over the years, I think my players and other women I've worked with have accepted me more than they might a lot of other men because they sense that I understand the role women have been forced to play and have tried to correct it. I became known early in my career as a very aggressive coach on the issue of equal opportunities for women athletes, and I've been proud to carry that label ever since. There have always been injustices toward women in sports, and I'm not bashful about standing up for equality.

Sometime during my second year at Pitt, I realized I was thinking of myself more as a coach than as a teacher; this was the profession I wanted to pursue. I lobbied with Cas Myslinski, the men's athletic director at Pitt, to create a men's program and merge the men's and women's coaching job. A year later, he did just that, hiring me to coach both teams — a full-time coaching job. Remarkably, my longtime passion was now my profession, and volleyball began to consume everything I did.

I was out of the classroom, but my schedule was no less crazy. I was paid $15,000 a year, about what I made as a high school teacher, and I ran camps and did a few clinics to augment my income, and I was also organizing the junior program. I liked having my own empire, knowing that the success or failure of the team depended on the way I organized things, independent of other people's mistakes. I thrive on making the tough calls, then taking all the yeas and nays that come with it. It gets to be pressured and burdensome at times, but that's what makes me go.

I also enjoyed working with young people. Young people keep me on my toes and keep me up to date. I've kept track of a few of those early Pitt players. Sue Hershelman played in Spain and later coached there. Cindy Chambers, the first player I ever recruited, turned up as an assistant coach at New Mexico State under Tom Shoji when I was at New Mexico. She's back in Philadelphia now, administering a cardiac rehabilitation program. I still talk with Cindy once in a while.

There are a few others I talk to from time to time, but I've lost track of most of them. Some coaches claim they keep track of every former player. I don't, and I'm a little skeptical of those who say they do. I don't feel the need to do that, and I don't think the players feel the need for it, either. One thing I do share with all my players, though: if anyone ever needed me for anything, or if I ever needed one of them, there'd be no questions asked. It would just be, "Yeah, let's get it done."

CHAPTER 7

GO WEST

I guess you'd call it itchy feet. As the '70s drew to a close, I'd accomplished about all I could at Pitt. We had built a program that won two regionals in a row, we had gotten the campus interested, and I had started a men's varsity team, but I was still making $15,000 per year, with little likelihood of further advancement. Our second daughter, Hillary, was born in 1977, so there were four of us and not very much money. Becky had asthma, and Pittsburgh was tough on asthma sufferers. And I always knew that ultimately I would like to get back to the Southwest if I got the chance.

I began to check into other coaching positions. I applied at the University of San Francisco, Texas A&M, and New Mexico. All three schools seemed interested, but the New Mexico people didn't write me or contact me for a long time. Then one day out of the blue I got a call from the associate athletic director there, saying if I was still interested they wanted to interview me.

I took to Albuquerque from the start. It reminded me of San Bernardino, very laid back. I immediately felt at home. I knew the lifestyle and it seemed like it would be fun to get back to it. I accepted the job to become head coach at New Mexico in 1980.

This was going to be a radically different challenge. At Pitt, we had built everything virtually from scratch. Whoever got that job after I left would have the advantage of building on what we'd established. By the same token, I was now coming into an established program. I wasn't going to have to reinvent the wheel. I inherited some solid athletes, and was able to recruit three very good players before heading west.

Shortly after I took the job, I got a call from Linda Estes, the athletic director. She told me she had several candidates for the assistant coaching position, including one she wanted to handle very carefully. Wanda Grissom was living with Gary Colson, New Mexico's basketball coach. Wanda had played volleyball at Pepperdine when Gary coached there. He had a houseboat in Marina Del Rey, and the two of them had set up housekeeping — houseboatkeeping? When Gary came to New Mexico to replace Norm Ellenberger, Wanda came with him.

So here was a former player from one of the nation's best volleyball schools moving to Albuquerque. She was a good candidate, but Linda wanted me to know the situation, because there couldn't be any hint of a package deal with Colson, particularly since Ellenberger had left New Mexico under a cloud. We couldn't have people asking, "Was part of the package for Colson that you had to hire his bunkmate?" It was a tricky dilemma, but after I screened all the candidates, it was clear Wanda was the best one for the job. That and nothing else made me hire her. She was my assistant coach for two years.

Wanda is now the director of group sales for the San Jose Sharks of the National Hockey League. She has another NHL connection, too: she's the stepdaughter of Bob Pulford, longtime general manager of the Chicago Blackhawks. When I first moved to Illinois, Wanda told me, "Listen, just call Bob and tell him who you are, and he'll set you up with boxes, whatever you want." I called him three times, never got through. I talked to a couple of assistants who said, "Oh, yeah, call him back tomorrow, he'd love to talk to you, I'm sure he'll fix you up," but we never hooked up. Maybe I'll try again one of these days; 10 years isn't too long to wait for hockey tickets, is it?

My first year at New Mexico we went 13-20, but came on really strong at the end of the season. We were in the Intermountain Athletic Conference, along with teams like Northern Arizona, Idaho State, Wyoming, Colorado State, Brigham Young, Utah, and Utah State. Arizona and Arizona State were also in the IAC before moving to the Pac-10. The Association for Intercollegiate Athletics for Women (AIAW) was still the national organization for women's sports, the NCAA not getting involved for another year, and the big challenge for us was to make the postseason AIAW tournament. If a team finished in the top six in the IAC's round-robin regular-season schedule, it qualified for the postseason tournament. We finished fifth that first year, and we set a goal of upsetting a higher-seeded team. In the first tournament match, we knocked off second-seeded Utah, depriving the Utes of a chance to go to the national tournament.

Then we lost to Colorado State, and I may have been partly to blame. Earlier during the tournament, I'd noticed one of Colorado State's setters, Sue Midland, having trouble with her serve. I just walked up and started working with her on her toss. Small world: after Sue graduated, the next time I saw her was 1988, when I was interviewing for a replacement for Don Hardin, my longtime assistant coach, who had just left Illinois for Louisville. I had breakfast with an applicant, and he brought his wife with him. The familiar face across the breakfast table was Sue's. Her husband, Jay Potter, is now a UI assistant coach.

After that first season at New Mexico, I was named to Chuck Erbe's World University Games staff and went to Romania for three weeks. That was an enormous opportunity for me, opening up a whole new arena. I'd always had a dream of helping to coach a national team and getting that USA warmup jacket, so when Chuck asked me to assist him, I was in heaven. Here I was at the USOC Training Center in Colorado Springs, on the staff of the head coach of the powerful USC team, one of volleyball's coaching legends. I was working with the country's best collegiate players, getting ready for a trip to Bucharest, where I'd see some of the best players in the world.

Not to slight the college game, but top international volleyball competition is light years beyond anything you'll ever see in a college match. We've had great teams at Illinois, we've seen the great teams at UCLA, Stanford, Hawaii — these teams would score maybe a couple of points against the strong international teams. The level of play is that much higher, in every way — hitting, blocking, passing, power, even the speed of the game. To be up close to that was a lot of fun for me, and quite an education, though a humbling one.

Our collegiate players went up against national teams from Cuba and China, two of the three best teams in the world, and it was like a good high school team playing an NCAA Final Four qualifier. We went out to warm up for our opening match, and I was giving our setters tosses. Remember, these are All-Americans, the best college players the United States had to offer. While we were in the middle of our warm-up, the Cuban coach walked out to the center of the net and started tossing quick sets to his players. Suddenly we were facing a steady, rapid-fire stream of leather. For every toss I got off, they must have hammered down 10 balls, right into the middle of our team.

Part of the international game involves probing your opponent for vulnerability, and if you find something that throws him off-balance, you keep it up. Well, the Cubans had gotten to us before the first whistle. We were gaping at these high-jumping, hard-hitting Cuban women — gaping and dodging. "Stand your ground," Chuck yelled at us from the bench. Sorry, Chuck — if we have but one life to give for our country, it's not going to be on the volleyball court.

That was an intimidating introduction to the international game, and it only got worse. The match started, we served the first ball, and we never got it back again. Fifteen-zip — a sideout and 15 straight points. OK, we get the message — we've got some ground to cover.

That trip catapulted my thinking to a higher level, and ever since, my association with the national program has been one of the most rewarding facets of my career. USA volleyball was in a stage of rapid development in 1981. Before the late '70s, the USA team had been run on a shoestring for decades, its teams tossed together just before a competition. But now both the men's and women's national teams were getting organized. The women went to Pasadena, Texas, the men to Dayton, Ohio, in two separate attempts to establish national training centers. During my time at Pitt, some of us would drive the 250 miles to Dayton to play in tournaments, and to watch them. The national program began developing different levels of teams. Besides the Olympic-level team, there were "B" teams, a junior national team, the Olympic Festival teams, the World University Games team. Now there's even a national elite training camp for high school-level players.

The organizational structure had come a long way, but there still was no national network in 1981 from which Chuck Erbe could put together a staff. The national program was just working off volunteer time, with a small pool of known coaching talent. My assignment to that first World University Games team just kind of happened. I had met Chuck through the American National Volleyball Association, which had emerged as a rival to the USVBA. Then Myles Gabel, who had been Chuck's assistant at USC for several years, moved to Albuquerque to work with a junior program. I met him there, and Myles recommended me to Chuck. I happened to be in the right place at the right time.

A few years later, after I got my feet on the ground at Illinois, I applied to become an Olympic Festival coach and was selected to be the head coach of the North team in 1985. I got to coach two of our own Illini players, Disa Johnson and Mary Eggers. The Festival itself was a great experience, and it was also an opportunity to interact with some of the great coaches — Dave Shoji was there, Rick Butler, Lisa Love, Debbie Brown. About the same time, Terry Liskeyvich, who'd just become the national team coach, asked me to serve as a consultant. He wanted to maintain roots in the college arena, and I was part of a large rotating group that included Andy Banachowski (UCLA), Terry Pettit (Nebraska), Kathy DeBoer (Kentucky), Jeff Mazzochi, who won a Division II national championship at Portland State, Lisa Love (USC), Jim Iams (Georgia), and Shelton Collier (Georgia Tech). That was a very good group to be involved with. We'd get together for meetings when we could, and we'd also go on national team trips — Canada, Cuba, Europe. Just being involved in that process kept ideas percolating.

I've found over the years that I function best coaching at that elite level. That's not to diminish what I've done with my college programs, but it really trips my switch to be at that top level, with the best athletes, coaching against the best. I do better with the athletes, I see the game better. One of my weaknesses is that I often don't have a great deal of patience for the rudimentary stages of training. If a player comes into my college program lacking a certain basic skill, I want to teach her, and I do, but sometimes my patience and my interest level wane.

I want to go to the chalkboard and jump to the next level. In fact, one of the warning signals I've learned to look for, if I have a team that's not getting any better under my coaching, is that I've become too fancy. I love tinkering with new concepts, and I always have to be on my guard against leaving my team behind. At the international level, though, those advanced concepts work.

From '85 on, I became more involved with the USA program. It's really been satisfying, and I'm grateful to Terry for encouraging me. Not only do you get to see the volleyball, but you get to travel to places most Americans never get to see, like

Cuba. I went to Cuba for the first of three trips in 1987. We were there for 10 days, playing five matches and traveling all over the island. We also spent a lot of time with the Cuban coaches, who were as much fun to be around as anyone I've ever known, just hilarious, great guys.

College players think that when they get to the national team, it's a big step up, and it is, on a competitive level. But in the places where we'd go to play, the style of living — the hotels, the food, schedules — isn't what our players are used to. That's one of the things that makes international competition challenging, of course, but it definitely takes some getting used to.

On my first trip to Cuba, we had to fly over from Miami on a little DC-3, on a charter service called Red Air. We sat in the airport in Miami for hours, and when they finally let us on the plane, some guy followed us on with a spray can, spraying the air and the aisles. I guess it was disinfectant, though we never found out for certain.

We hopped over to Havana and sat in that airport for about six hours, trying to keep track of our group's bags. People were running around everywhere, everyone speaking Spanish, of course, which none of us understood very well. About midnight, a truck pulled up and some soldiers hauled our bags in. They drove us into town, where we checked into a hotel and finally had a meal, at about 1 a.m. Then we all went up to our rooms, and we were asleep for an hour and a half when the phone rang: we had to get up, go back to the airport and fly to Santiago de Cuba, which, as it turned out, is where we were supposed to play, not Havana. So we loaded everything back into the truck and went back to the airport — and waited for another four hours. It seemed the plane wasn't full yet. They didn't really follow a flight schedule, they just waited until the plane filled up and then took off, kind of like the taxis in Nigeria.

We got to Santiago de Cuba, which is the garrison where Castro organized the revolution — they've preserved the bullet holes in the house where he was when Batista's army came after him. I had studied Cuban history, so it was fascinating for me, though maybe not so much for the athletes. We arrived there, and sat on the steps of *that* airport for another 6 1/2 hours, until finally a rickety old bus came for us. Had they forgotten about us? Who knows? That's just it — in international settings like that, you don't know what happens, why you're not picked up, why you *are* picked up, it just happens. Anyway, that was our first day and a half in Cuba, and that's not atypical of the international experience.

I'm not sure that's a bad thing, either. In the States, the players fly in comfort, ride in luxurious, air-conditioned buses, check into the Marriott and order familiar foods from room service. And everything is done right on schedule — practices, matches, buses, flights — just about every event of the tour is on a timetable; just be there on time, and everything goes smoothly. The foreign trips demand some flexibility, some adaptability from the athletes that they can translate to obstacles they might encounter on the court, or in life. The hardships trim away the people who don't have discipline and focus. If you learn nothing else, you learn to always expect a screw-up, always expect to be thrown off schedule.

Of course, we learned a lot about the world, too, particularly about the parts most Americans had no access to. We always felt much safer in the Soviet-bloc countries than in Western Europe. In France or West Germany or Belgium or Holland, anything could happen, from anti-American demonstrations to terrorist attacks. In Cuba, Romania, Yugoslavia, Czechoslovakia, no one got out of line. The price of freedom, I guess, but when we came back from behind the Iron Curtain, people would say, "Oh, you had to go to Romania?" as if that was something frightening. I'd say, "No, it was great — I could wear a USA warm-up without worrying about being attacked."

That was always a danger anywhere else in the world. In fact, we'd tell our athletes, "Don't wear USA paraphernalia, don't identify yourself as Americans." In the socialist countries, though, they know who you are, they know what their job is, and they know how to protect you. I think, too, that the people in the socialist countries somehow knew better how to distinguish between a government and its people. They knew volleyball players weren't involved in making foreign policy. In Western Europe and other parts of the "free world," some people seem to have trouble making that distinction.

USA volleyball has been an ongoing education, a really big part of my personal growth through the years. Not just the travel, but the association with the players and coaches — and not just our coaches in the USA program, but coaches all over the world. I can pick up a phone now and call a volleyball coach in Cuba or Japan or Germany, wherever.

Since about 1987, I've had a serious interest in becoming the Olympic coach. Not because I want to leave Illinois or my players, not that I'm unhappy, but because that is, very simply, the best job in the land, working at the highest level of the sport. It's not anything that's consuming me, but if that were ever to become an opportunity, I'd be very interested in looking at it. Right now, Terry Liskeyvich has been coaching the team since '85, and he just signed up for his third term, so the job hasn't been available. I'm still part of Terry's consulting staff, and as long as he'll have me, I'll coach another USA team at some level, I'll continue to go on national team trips, I'll continue to evaluate talent at the major tryouts. And after 1996, if I have the energy and the desire to stay in coaching, I'll probably announce my interest in the Olympic position.

What a great experience it's been to be involved with the U.S. team, and that first trip to the World University Games set the tone. Traveling to Romania, seeing the world's best players together in one place, training in an Olympic-style village — the whole atmosphere of international competition was a thrill for a guy getting ready to start his sixth year of coaching. I went there and brought back all that experience, and a couple of weeks later, my own team started to train at New Mexico.

The first year, we had done better than people expected us to. In '81, we were 26-17 and had some really big wins, surprising a lot of teams by playing them tough. At Pitt, I had always been aware of the West Coast teams' anti-East Coast bias. The attitude was that there just wasn't any volleyball east of Las Vegas. Well, Albuquerque isn't very far east of Las Vegas, but New Mexico was still a victim of that bias, particularly since the school had hired a coach from an Eastern school. It felt awfully good to go west and win.

The headiest part of that season started with a match against Pepperdine at Malibu. I remember everything about that match, right down to the pregame warm-up. We got to the gym early, but nothing was set up yet. Gary Sato, the women's coach, and Marv Dunphy, the men's coach at the time, and a couple of guys from the men's team were on the floor, playing basketball. They gave us a nonchalant greeting, then went on with their game. We just leaned against the wall, waiting for their volleyball coaches to stop playing basketball so we could get on the floor.

Go West 75

That was OK, though, because once they cleared the court and put up the net, we smoked 'em, three games to none. Man, what a sweet win. Chuck Erbe had driven up for the match from his home in Huntington Beach, and I was proud to have my World University Games "mentor" in the stands to see us beat Pepperdine.

At Pitt, we'd had some pretty good wins, but we rarely got to play the top teams. In 1978, we played Pacific, which was ranked third in the nation. We eventually lost the match, but we had them down 12-3 in the first game. They were stunned, like, "Who are those guys?" Beating Pepperdine in Malibu was a milestone for me, a big win at a new school against an established Top 10 team. And it started a West Coast trip where we showed we could do it again.

After beating Pepperdine, we drove to Santa Barbara and lost to UCSB. Then back into the cars for the drive to San Luis Obispo, a loss to Cal Poly. Then on to Palo Alto, where we lost to Stanford, and San Jose for a win over San Jose State. After the West Coast tour, we were ranked 12th in the nation, completely out of nowhere. We didn't know what to make of it.

We came back home and continued to win and to stay in the spotlight. We earned an at-large berth in the inaugural NCAA volleyball tournament, drawing Miami of Ohio for a first-round home match. We played at The Pit, the basketball arena, drawing more than 3,000 fans and astonishing everyone with the size of the crowd. It was a big deal, because it was rare then to have a New Mexico team in an NCAA tournament, *any* NCAA tournament. We won our first-round match and headed to the regional, eventually losing to San Diego State, which went on to beat Brigham Young and reach the national finals. After the season, I was named IAC Coach of the Year.

In 1982, we were just over .500, but we had a pretty good team. It was similar to the 1990 and 1991 Illinois teams, talented but easily distracted, not mature enough to create the chemistry to play together.

That was a tough time for me, a time of personal up-heaval, but a very valuable time. Anna and I had split up, and I had met Sherry Bedeaux, who would eventually become my second wife. Anna and I separated in January of 1981, but the divorce was held up legally for three years, just a nightmare of lawyers. The law is absolutely prejudicial against the male in divorce proceedings. I will stand before any feminist group in the world and, without blinking an eye, make that statement.

The breakup of the marriage dropped me back into poverty, too. After the separation, I moved into an apartment with three plates, two forks and a spoon. I remember my daughter Becky hated to go into the kitchen and see how bare it was. She'd make me go to garage sales, where I'd buy a frying pan for 50 cents or something like that. I slept on the floor until I saved up enough to get a bed, and I bought a folding couch for the kids to sleep on when they visited. It was grim. And all the while, I was going through hell with my ex-wife and the attorneys.

Apart from the stress of my separation and divorce, the way I looked at the world was changing in other ways. The student radical had grown older, the heat of the political fires that had raged inside had begun to cool. Not my belief in the principles — that was solid — but the zeal with which I built my daily life around those principles subsided. I began to let a little more of myself come to the surface. I started playing volleyball again, I took up skiing, played a lot of golf, just made the most of being in a recreation-oriented environment. I started letting my hair down, I started living.

Professionally, my time at New Mexico made me realize that my success at Pittsburgh hadn't been an accident. I saw that I could do it again, build a program and have success. I could figure out a way for this group of people to play this schedule against these teams and score enough points to win and get a little better in the process, so they'd be ready for the next team on the schedule.

And I began to realize that that was part of why I'd become a coach. I've always loved athletics. I think athletics can provide some of the most noble and challenging experiences a person can ever confront, and I say that having confronted some heavy challenges in my life. The experiences athletes have in competition can provide the skills to face adversity for the rest of their lives. I know first-hand what athletics can do for a person — success in sports was one of the building blocks for the self-confidence and self-esteem that were so hard for me to find after losing my father.

Through the years I've become more and more proud to be part of the coaching profession. Many people seem to assume anyone involved professionally with athletics is a knucklehead who discovered he couldn't do anything else. Let's tackle, let's block, let's run wind sprints — that's the extent of the life. I'm not sure where that attitude comes from, but I've been a college professor, a high school teacher, I have a Ph.D. — I've been around the educational world — and I can say without a shadow of a doubt that the people I've met in athletics on the whole are more aware and brighter in the way they carry out their jobs than most of the people I've met in the academic world. College professors tend to be fairly myopic, thinking the world revolves around their particular discipline, but they enjoy a lofty position of respect in our society. Coaches, on the other hand, are some of the most creative, hard-working, tough-minded people I know, but their reputation doesn't reflect that.

A lot of people in the media and in society in general feel the freedom to tee off on coaches and athletes. Pick up the paper, listen to the news reports, and you'll find that people just assume athletes aren't smart. I don't know where that started. I've never seen it. The athletes I coach are smarter for the most part than the students I used to teach in college, and if you look at their grade-point averages as a whole, they're at least on a par if not higher than the general student body's.

The universities themselves express the same prejudicial perspective. Try this sometime: suggest to a university administrator that a student-athlete should get academic credit for his athletic pursuits. I can almost guarantee that administrator will react as though you're crazy or stupid or both. But that student is on scholarship because of his or her skill in a performing art, just the same as the person with a music scholarship or a drama scholarship. Yet those people follow a curriculum to study music or drama, and they get academic credit for that. I don't see why an athlete can't do that. It would be easy to build a curriculum around the athlete's experience, from the psychology and the science of it to the marketing and promotions and business end of it. The same spectrum of topics that can be applied to any other performing art can be applied to athletics.

But there's a built-in anti-athletics mentality. The assumption behind the term "student-athlete" is that while you're performing as an athlete, you're not being a student. But when a drama person is performing as an actor, he *is* being a student. I don't understand that. I don't know where it started, the notion that athletic activity is less worthwhile. I know the things my athletes do when I'm coaching them are very sophisticated, very demanding, and require maturity and discipline. In athletics we build on principles, like learning how to face difficulties and work with different groups and overcome obstacles, lifelong principles that are engendered in the athletic arena maybe better than anyplace else. It's a wonderful learning environment.

Coaches are primarily teachers, the difference between us and a classroom professor being that we're held accountable for whether we teach the skills or we don't, as expressed in winning and losing. We're accountable to the administration, which tends to let you go if you lose and keep you on when you win. I look over at the academic side of the university, and I don't see anyone checking up on the political science professor to see how many of her students get A's. In that arena, if the student fails, it's the student's fault; if the student does well, it's because the professor's a great teacher.

Coaches are the pincushions of the university. We take it from every direction. We don't have the security of tenure, just the reverse. We're asked to make sure our athletes do well in the classroom, and I do. I talk academics all the time with my athletes, I work with them on writing skills, reading skills, I get them into the study halls and monitor their work at all times. Does the biology professor have any responsibility to the student once he leaves the lab?

Sometimes people say, "Coach, I heard you on the radio last night — it sure is good to hear a coach who's articulate and intelligent." I always want to respond, "Just what are you saying? What do you mean? That, in contrast to me, most coaches are uneducated fools?" To me it's like saying, "Some of my best friends are Negroes." Whites used to say that to blacks, not realizing what a condescending insult it was. Don't people realize it's an insult to say that to me? I feel very close to my colleagues in athletics. Meet Illinois' football coach, Lou Tepper, basketball coach Lou Henson, and tell me these aren't some of the finest people you'd ever want to be around in your life — people who stand for the right things, who are extremely intelligent, who can make decisions on their feet, who'll never weasel out when it's time to be loyal. I could give you a litany of the principles and character these people have, people whose profession is sports.

Sport, at its best, is an enterprise in integrity. Put two teams in a gym, athletes, coaches — take the crowd out, the press, everything else — and you've got something terrific. People can screw it up — athletes, coaches, referees, promoters — people can contaminate it. But in its pure form, sport has a beauty to it, a truth. And that truth can happen over and over again. There's always a result to it, it's clear who wins and loses, what your time was in the 100. Sport provides a clarity that everyone craves.

A friend of mine from the Peace Corps, Bill Barich (he of the Dick Barnett jump shot), is a novelist, and one of his books, *Laughing in the Hills*, is about the world of horse racing and handicapping. The main character finds fulfillment in this environment, and he finally concludes that it's because the handicapper is responsible for his own success or failure. He studies the *Racing Form*, develops his own theories about past performance, learns what significance to attach to doping, and then when the bets are all in, there's a perfectly unambiguous resolution.

When I read that novel, I realized that a lot of what I like about coaching can be couched in the same philosophy. I love the clarity of it. I don't have to rely on anyone's opinion of me. I can call my own shots and do whatever I want in the creation of the product. That is extremely appealing, and I never had that option in any other profession. Even in teaching, you have your own classroom, but there's always a chance the legislature will dictate a curriculum change in social studies. In coaching, I write my own curriculum.

At New Mexico I had learned that I could write a winning curriculum at the college level, that my success at Pitt was something I could take with me to other programs. I knew I wanted to keep coaching, to confront new challenges, and I knew I was good at it. Then suddenly a call came that would allow me to test this newfound confidence, a siren call from a school in the Midwest: "Come on, give this a shot. Let's see what you've got."

TALKING TRASH

"You know," I told Karol Kahrs, "I'm going to quit as a volleyball coach and just hire myself out to any university that will bring me in for a year or two." The '83-84 school year was coming to an end, and I was shooting the breeze with Illinois' associate athletic director for women's sports.

I had come to the UI the previous August, and the Illini football team promptly won its first Big Ten championship in 20 years and went to the Rose Bowl. The basketball team shared the Big Ten title and advanced to the NCAA regional finals. It was the continuation of a pattern: I always brought a school good athletic luck in my first year. In 1976, I'd shown up on the Pitt campus, and Johnny Majors led the Panthers to the national football championship behind Tony Dorsett. Shortly after I moved to New Mexico in 1980, Joe Morrison was Coach of the Year after directing the football team to a 10-1 record and the WAC title. Now I had come to Illinois, and bam — Rose Bowl and Big Ten basketball title. What was the volleyball team's record, you ask? Let's not talk about that right now.

I hadn't been Illinois' first choice. Following the 1982 season, Dr. Kahrs wanted to make a coaching change, to bring in one of the big guns in volleyball. Chuck Erbe had as much to do with my being hired as anyone. Karol had contacted Chuck, Pacific's Terry Liskeyvich and a number of the nation's other top coaches. Some of them came to Champaign for interviews, and she decided she wanted Chuck. But he deliberated for quite a while, then finally declined.

Karol was disappointed not to get Chuck for the job, of course, but it was even worse that so much time had passed while she was waiting for his decision. Now it would be tough to find anyone else. I think she must have said something like, "Doggone it, Chuck, now that you've taken all my time and you're going to decline, you've got to help me out." Chuck gave her my name as a possibility, and when Karol contacted me, it set me thinking.

Illinois? I didn't know anything about the place. Never in my wildest dreams had Illinois entered into my coaching plans. Chuck tried to do some pump priming, inviting Sherry and me down to play golf one day and dropping hints about the UI job. Illinois appealed to my professional ambitions — the salary structure, the benefits, the organization. New Mexico had been an improvement over my situation at Pitt, and this was another step up the ladder. And from my time at Indiana, I knew all about the academic reputation of the Big Ten Conference. I knew this was a place with tradition.

Still, here I was in 1983, having just returned "home" from the East Coast a few years before. I wasn't thrilled about moving to the Midwest. Anna and I were divorced, and I didn't want to leave my children. Then, too, I wasn't sure how Sherry would feel about a move.

I had met Sherry after Anna and I separated. In fact, Wanda Grissom introduced us. Wanda worked part-time at a restaurant in Albuquerque, the Rio Grande Yacht Club, where Sherry also worked. The early months with Sherry were on again, off again. The moment of truth came when I decided to pursue the Illinois job. Would Sherry come with me or not? In fact, that question came astonishingly close to spiking my chances for the job.

I was sitting at breakfast with Karol Kahrs discussing my plans. I mentioned that Sherry and I would probably get a place together and that we were trying to figure out whether to get married or not. That was a completely normal conversation to have where I was living, but Karol practically choked on her cereal. At a later meeting with Karol, she told me, "I had to use the last couple of hours to decide whether I wanted to continue the interview or not." She was utterly knocked off balance by the fact that a coach would come in and live with a woman without being married. "The fact that you were honest about it worked in your favor," Karol said. I'd been honest, sure, but mainly I'd been completely unaware that was the sort of thing that could cost me the job.

Talking Trash 83

Sherry is perfect for me, by the way. While developing her own successful career as an educator in the Urbana Public Schools, she has skillfully and graciously managed the beyond-the-call-of-duty responsibilities of the wife of a successful and visible coach. The receptions at our home, entertaining recruits and their parents, the long hours accompanying me on trips, the countless interruptions in our personal lives, her willingness to chat with parents and boosters while waiting for me to free myself from meetings and interviews—she has handled all of this and more in an unselfish manner. Ultimately Sherry made an honest man of me, marrying me in 1984 on the President's Lawn at the UI. We had our reception in the Varsity Room. Now, finally, we were respectable, living in sin no longer.

That view of morality was just one of many ways in which the mindset of the Southwest is different from Champaign's. I remember talking to Jan LaDuke, Karol's secretary, when I was setting up my interview in Champaign, asking whether I should bring dress shorts or not. She thought it was a joke, but in Albuquerque, when people dress up at night it means putting on a clean polo shirt or a Hawaiian shirt with dress shorts. Instead of flip-flops, you might wear sandals. As a kid in Southern California, I had a pair of tattered shorts, a pair of school shorts and a pair of formal shorts, and it was the same with shirts. It was all people wore. When I went back to the West, I reverted to my childhood ways of thinking about dress.

After she realized I was serious, Jan patiently explained that I would need a jacket and a tie. I owned no tie, no jacket. People don't wear that stuff in Albuquerque. I came to Champaign in a borrowed coat and a tie during a July heat wave, humidity about 90 percent. The first thing I did in my interview was take off the jacket. After a while, I said, "Karol, I can't wear this tie," and she said, "Oh, it's really hot, don't worry about it." I remember living for the moment when we could leave a meeting and get into her air-conditioned car and drive somewhere. Coming from the driest climate in the country, I was melting.

I honestly hadn't come to Champaign expecting to take the job. I owed it to myself to take a look, but I thought I'd look it over and move on. But once I got to Champaign, I saw a lot of sound, logical reasons to take the job. Here was a school with a great academic reputation, located in the middle of a sizable triangle of population defined by Chicago, St. Louis and Indianapolis. That meant a large recruiting pool and a strong possibility of attracting great talent. The UI athletic programs weren't competing with anything else for attention in Champaign-Urbana, no minor league baseball, no CBA team. The community support would come if I could get the program going.

Maybe most important, Karol and athletic director Neale Stoner promised me a full commitment to volleyball, and they delivered. Stoner had little face-to-face participation in my hiring, though clearly he was the one who made the decision to spend a little more money on the program. I didn't get all the right numbers on my first visit to Illinois, but that commitment has always remained over the last decade. Neale and Karol didn't know how much money it would take, but when I explained to them after my first year what we'd need, they didn't give me a song-and-dance, they gave me support. Every time that a critical move has needed to be made, it has been done. I've never had administrators at every turn saying, "Oh, God, we'll never do that, we can't afford to do that."

Neale took some hits later over Illinois' problems with the NCAA, and some people in the community are still bitter toward him, but he really knew how to generate enthusiasm around the program. There never was a staff meeting where he didn't have a model of a new building or a new part of the five-year plan or a motto like "The '80s belong to the Illini" — that was good stuff. He fired up all the boosters because he talked their language. He'd walk into a luncheon and say, "Hey, dammit, we're on the move here, and if you don't like it, step aside, let us through, because we're on the move, and by the way, we need a check for about $5,000, but I'll tell you what, we get that check from you, you'll never be sorry, 'cause anytime you're hanging around us, we're going to show you a damn good time."

When I asked myself how far I could go at New Mexico, I saw that Illinois, with its location and its academic reputation, offered a better opportunity for the great players I'd need to build an elite program. New Mexico has a wonderful charm and more academic strengths than most people might realize, but there are certain schools universally recognized as academically solid, and Illinois is one of those schools. It was clear to me that Illinois represented a step onto firmer ground in every aspect of my profession.

Talking Trash

After several weeks of deliberation, I took the job. The timing was awkward, because I had just signed six players to come to New Mexico. I was doing an elite camp in Pueblo, Colorado, and I had to send telegrams to everyone at New Mexico, including my players, to give them the news. I think parents, athletes, and administrators sometimes assume that coaches control these scenarios. But jobs open up and answers have to be made on a timetable completely out of our control, and all we can do is try to be fair to everyone and deal with the pressures exacted by the process.

It's especially tricky when you're trying to learn all you need to know about the new place before making this enormous commitment. I might ask 11 questions and get answers to nine. So maybe they tell me, "We don't really know about those two issues, but we'll get back to you tomorrow." Tomorrow turns into Friday, and Friday turns into next Friday, and suddenly your neat little timetable to make sure you didn't offend anyone is obliterated, and people think you're stringing them along, and you're offending everyone you see.

I really had made a point of asking questions when I'd been to Champaign for my interview, and Karol was tireless in answering them. She and I stayed up one night until about 5:30 a.m., going over a list of questions I had written out, and she answered every one she could. I wanted everything gone over, every "t" crossed and every "i" dotted. But even with all my questions, I wasn't quite prepared for what I found when I arrived in Champaign in early August, just two days before the team showed up for practice.

When we flew in, Karol met Sherry and me at the airport, along with her friends Bill and Doris Higgins, two of the program's earliest boosters. We spent our first night at Karol's house because our furniture hadn't arrived at our little condominium yet. Poor Sherry had to get the whole house together while I went off and coached.

My assistant coach, Don Hardin, showed up the next day and we went to check out Kenney Gym. I knew coming in that I'd find things in disarray, but now I realized that, with the long list of questions I'd asked on my visit, I hadn't bothered to examine the facility where my team would play. Neale Stoner hadn't been in town when I visited, so Karen Iehl-Morse, a trainer, had walked me around campus, along with assistant AD Tom Porter. Karen wasn't even going to be the volleyball trainer, but she was the only person available. She took me to Kenney, but we didn't actually tour the building. She just pointed at it and we walked in for a few minutes and then got out. Now I could see why.

Kenney Gym was the worst facility I had ever seen or heard about. We had no locker room, but that was the least of our problems. The place was filthy, scum everywhere. There were pads around the girders that were nothing but coat hangers wrapped around old mattresses. We found maggots crawling in one of them. Windows were broken out in the gym, leaves were scattered everywhere and the floor hadn't had any attention in who knows how many decades. There was stuff hanging on the walls that I can't describe because I can't begin to guess what it was.

It was 1983, but there had to be junk in Kenney that had been there since the place was built in 1900. And everything there was either broken, worn out or rotting. It was also a notorious center of campus crime. Students didn't want to go near Kenney, and teachers didn't want to teach there. There had been rapes reported there, and all sorts of theft. And this, mind you, is where I was supposed to build my Big Ten powerhouse.

Well, I'm the volleyball coach, so my first priority was finding the volleyball equipment. All the volleyball equipment, I was told, was in "the volleyball box." A storage room? No, a box. Finally they showed me: a padlocked plywood box on wheels, about 2 1/2 feet high and four feet long. Inside was everything the Fighting Illini volleyball program owned. One problem: the box had been kicked in during the summer and the contents had been stolen. Welcome to your new job, your step up the professional ladder.

Don and I looked at each other, and we didn't know whether to laugh or cry. We had *nothing*, no ball, no net, no place to store anything securely if we'd *had* a ball and net. I have no idea how John Blair, my predecessor, had run that program, or how anybody could have run that program. Often when a program fails, it's a circumstantial problem more than a coaching problem. The state of UI volleyball wasn't John Blair's fault. He didn't have anywhere near the budget or support that I would have. Volleyball had been at the bottom of the Illini totem pole.

We held our first few practices at the Intramural and Physical Education Building; at least there we could check out a net and a ball. Then, once we'd removed the first layer of filth, we moved to Kenney, home of Fighting Illini volleyball. We were in

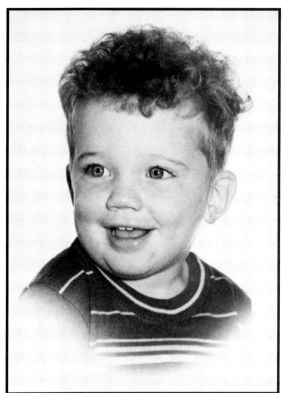

Here I am at the tender age of two, ready for all the world's challenges.

This is one of the few pictures I have of my father, Captain Robert R. Hebert. I'm the one with the glasses. My younger brother, Rich, is in front, and my sister, Pam, is on the right. Pam was killed in an auto accident in 1967 when she was just 21 years old.

My athletic career began to take flight in high school, where I played point guard on the San Bernardino High School basketball team. This picture was taken during my senior year in 1961, when I was named third team all-conference.

My service as a Peace Corps worker in Africa provided some of the most exciting and rewarding times of my life. At right I'm shown with Maureen (center), the Canadian volunteer whose place I took in 1966, and Francis (right), the steward who assisted me during my stay in Nigeria. Below is a picture of me in 1966 with the principal (front row, third from the right) and a group of students from St. John's Teacher Training College in Diobu, Nigeria.

I'm busy at my desk in 1974 as an assistant professor at Chatham College, my first professional position after graduate school.

Kathy Hudgins (25) and Patricia "Stretch" Montgomery (13) helped lead my first team at Pittsburgh in 1976.

Here I am "making my point" to Sue Garcia (10) and Teri Nielson (8) during the 1981 season at New Mexico.

Since coming to Illinois in 1983, I've been fortunate to receive tremendous support from my coaches, players, and the athletic administration. My long-time assistant coach Don Hardin (left) now serves as the head women's volleyball coach at the University of Louisville.

Associate Director of Athletics Dr. Karol Kahrs gave us the full support of the Athletic Department as we built the Illinois women's volleyball program into a national power.

Mary Eggers, who starred for the Illini from 1985-88, was the best competitor I have ever coached.

Our success in the NCAA tournament has been the measuring stick for the progress of our program. I remember the feeling of complete joy and satisfaction when we walked off the Kenney Gym court in 1988 (above) after beating Oklahoma to advance to the Final Four in Minneapolis. Last year's match against Stanford in the NCAA regional final at Huff Gym (below) was one of the greatest matches I have ever been involved in.

Illini All-American Kirsten Gleis was one of the finest athletes ever to attend the University of Illinois. Her tremendous skill and leadership keyed our 34-4 record for the 1992 season.

Being named college volleyball's national Coach of the Year in 1985 was a proud moment for me and the Illinois program.

The Illinois coaching braintrust goofs around during the 1991 season. With me are current Illini assistants Jay Potter (left) and Disa Johnson (right). Kathy Cunningham (second from left), who served as our graduate assistant coach for the 1991 season, is now the head coach at the University of Wisconsin-Milwaukee.

The Old Guys Golf and Ski Club (OGGS) has a rotating roster of about 20 guys who have gotten together since 1980 to play in "masters" volleyball tournaments around the county. Shown above, the squad reunited for the 1990 U.S. Volleyball Association tournament in Toledo, Ohio. Left to right: Jim Graham, Deek Smith, Bill Florentine, Monte McBride, me, Mel Goralski, Buzz Schwartz.

I celebrated Christmas 1991 with my brother, Rich, and my mother, Lola, at my brother's home in Crestline, California.

This picture of my family was taken during the summer of 1993, shortly after my daughter Becky graduated from the University of Illinois. From left to right, the Hebert family includes Hillary, who is a high school sophomore in New Mexico; my wife, Sherry; me; and Becky.

Talking Trash

the middle of our first practice there when a bell rang. Suddenly students started coming out of classrooms and walking right across the gym floor, right through our practice. We were conducting practice for a varsity athletic program, but we might as well have been invisible. Students strolled by, chatting and laughing with one another, and if they noticed us at all, they acted as though we were in their way. The players didn't think anything about it. Generations of players had seen generations of students walk through generations of practices; it was the closest thing Illini volleyball had to a tradition. Don and I, on the other hand, were dumbfounded.

The next day, Don and I headed to the Memorial Stadium to tell Bulldog Wright in the Maintenance Office about our problem. He seemed eager to help.

"Hey, fellas," he said, "no problem. Come on over here. I got something for you. You ever seen one of these?" He held up a piece of plywood in the shape of an H. He seemed very proud of it, but we didn't know what to make of it. Literally. He handed me the plywood. "You hold onto that and follow me. You ever seen any of this?" A big coil of nylon rope. We started to get the feeling we were being strung along. "You take this rope," he said, "and you wrap it around that spool. Then you take it over there to your gym, and you tie the rope around the pillars to make a little fence. That'll keep your practice safe."

OK, fine, that's what we'd do. We took this stupid piece of nylon rope, tied it all the way around the court. Next day, we were in practice, the bell rang — and people tore down the rope and walked across the floor just like before.

It seems funny now, but at that point Don and I were seriously questioning whether we had done the right thing in coming to Illinois. It was irritating having our practices interrupted, of course, but it was the attitude that the interruptions conveyed that really got to us, the complete campus-wide lack of respect for the program. It was insulting. Would people have strolled across Mike White's football practice field? Would Lou Henson's basketball practices ever suffer such annoyances? We were starting so low, we honestly weren't sure accomplishing what we wanted to accomplish would be possible.

Everyone we called for practice space or equipment seemed annoyed that we were bothering them. You want a chair? You want a trash can? Just for volleyball? I lived in a constant state of complete and utter frustration and anger at Kenney Gym. But we didn't give up, we kept on pushing for the bare minimum of facilities for a varsity program.

We wanted to practice on Saturdays and some evenings, but we couldn't reserve time in our own gym. I found out that, in an unofficial public relations gesture, as a way of throwing a few crumbs to the community, the university had essentially designated Kenney Gym as an open gym. Kenney was the DMZ, an unofficial buffer zone between the university and the community. I would plead my case with university people that Kenney should be closed to everyone but UI students and faculty, but I got nowhere.

I got into the habit of stopping by Kenney when I was out and about to see what was going on in my volleyball home. One night at about 2 a.m., when Sherry and I were on our way home from a party, I walked into the gym and saw the balcony filled with teen-agers, smoking cigarettes — I don't know what kind — and drinking beer. They'd obviously been there some time — brown bags and empty bottles were strewn everywhere. On the floor, kids were riding their bicycles, leaving skid marks on our court. In another part of the gym, kids were using an old PE climbing rope to swing out from the balcony and drop onto some pads they'd ripped off the walls. All the lights were on. No security. No nothing. Not one person in that building was remotely connected to the university. People screaming, drinking alcohol, smoking, riding bicycles, doing God knows what else, just utter chaos — at 2 in the morning. Our volleyball team couldn't get our own gym reserved, but anyone else in the free world could get into the gym, and nobody was going to tell them not to.

And that was our home, that was where our program was asked to live. That's what I'd tell people: "Listen, I live there, my team lives there, and we won't tolerate that existence."

One of our biggest victories came when we got a blue curtain hung around the practice floor to separate it from the corridor where the students would emerge from classes. Oh, what a difference that made: a physical boundary that said, "This is our space — if you don't belong here, stay out." Of course, when it first went up, people would walk through the curtain, people who had been walking across that floor for years after class, and their brothers and sisters for years before them. But we wouldn't let them get away with it. A student would wander into our practice, and Don and I would stop him and make him walk around. Students must have thought we were the biggest jerks on campus. They were simply doing what every student had done for years, walking through Kenney Gym. But the word must have gotten out about the new crazy volleyball coaches, because gradually the problem disappeared.

We were making a point, and our players loved it. "God," they said, "we've never had anybody stand up for us." That was a big deal for them: they were never going to get any respect on campus, or from other teams, if they didn't respect themselves, and it was a lot easier for them to respect themselves if they knew their coaches respected them and believed in them, and were willing to fight for them. As for Don and me, we were staking out our turf. If this was all they were going to give us, we were by God going to hold onto it and do the best we could with it.

After the curtain, we got iron covers for the basketball goals so people could come in and shoot hoops only during specified hours. We got a full-time security guard. We got the floor redone. We went through hell to get a locker room. We got the gym painted. We got scoreboards, that took a while. We got new pads to replace the disgusting, moth-eaten old mattresses and gymnastics pads wrapped around the pillars so people wouldn't skull themselves. They'd never had a public address system, and we finally got that. All this took about five years, bit by bit.

And it was every bit as hard to get rid of things we didn't need at Kenney as it was to get things we needed. There was a kickboxing practice apparatus someone had left there years before. There was netting on the north wall that the baseball team had used for indoor batting practice once upon a time. Nobody ever used the stuff anymore, and we kept asking Space Utilization, the people officially in charge of the building, "Who do we see about getting this trash hauled away?" "Can't move that," they'd say. "That's baseball's. That has to stay — belongs to that kickboxer."

We asked Tom Dedin, the baseball coach, "Tom, do you use this stuff?" "I don't even know what it is," he said. "I've never seen it." We tried to track down the kickboxer and found out he'd left campus 10 years before. But all that trash had to stay where it was; Kenney Gym was the UI's unofficial white elephant's graveyard, where useless junk went to die. One day, some workers came in to replace a boiler in the basement, using a trap door on the floor. They ripped apart the wooden crating from their new boiler and just tossed the scraps in a corner, where they stayed for six weeks. Kenney Gym was one big garbage can, and it was clear that no one but us gave a damn.

Finally, Don and I snapped. One Sunday night, we met at the gym and dragged everything we could find that wasn't being used anymore out into a hallway. It took us hours, but we cleared every stick out of there, and by the time we finished, you literally couldn't get through that hallway. Someone was going to do something with all this stuff now, or else they were going to have to seal that hallway off forever. When the deed was done, we grabbed a beer and speculated about what would happen. Would we face the wrath of Space Utilization? Would our pile of trash become a campus landmark? Then the worst possible scenario hit us: would someone come and put everything right back where it had been? We shuddered at the thought, and had another beer.

The next day, we went to practice and the pile was gone, every scrap thrown away. I guess the maintenance staff had come to the gym that morning and found our big pile of junk. They couldn't have known anything about it except what their eyes and common sense told them: it was trash. "Hey, we got a bunch of crap in the hallway — we're gonna need a truck." It must have taken them hours to load the stuff into a truck and haul it away, but all that mattered to us was that it was gone. Don and I exchanged secret smiles. This is the first time the truth about the Great Kenney Cleanup Caper has been revealed.

Flushed by the success of that covert action, we next undertook the Great Wastebasket Affair. Kenney had these old wire mesh wastebaskets that had been made in about 1837. They were all beaten up and bent up, they looked like hell, and to top it off they didn't hold anything — trash would just fall right through the mesh. It was bad enough we had to live with these sorry excuses for wastebaskets, but it was downright embarrassing to have our fans see them.

Whenever we'd try to requisition wastebaskets, we were told the same thing: "If there's a wastebasket there, we can't replace it." I put Don in charge of wastebasket replacement. We'd have a staff meeting, and Don would say, "Mike, no, no, don't make me call the wastebasket office, please, please." He'd come back from his confrontation a broken man. "Listen, sonny," they'd tell him, "wastebaskets are at a premium at this here university. Not everybody gets new wastebaskets; you just have to make do with the ones you've got." Every six months or so I'd have Don call the wastebasket office and let them rebuff him. "I thought I told you last year, sonny, you're not getting any new wastebaskets."

We finally snapped on this one, too. Don and I collected all the wastebaskets and took them down into the catacombs of Kenney Gym. We just kept going and going until we ran out of real estate, back into an old deserted locker area where no human had set foot in decades. We found an old trap door, way in the corner of the farthest reaches of this locker area — below the swimming pool, I think — and we took our old wastebaskets and just winged 'em back there as far as we could. The next day, Don called the wastebasket office. "I don't know how to tell you this, but the wastebaskets at Kenney Gym have been stolen." Three days later, we had brand new cans. The old ones will probably be discovered by archaeologists in 2100, and they'll puzzle over the primitive beings who would ever have used such stupidly de-signed things.

FROM LESS THAN ZERO

In January 1988, Don Hardin and I were on a ski trip with our wives, tooling across a long stretch of road in Colorado about 3 or 4 in the morning. I had a tape recorder running, and we were thinking out loud. In five years, we had taken a team from last place to the NCAA semifinals. "Give me one sentence," I told Don, "that makes sense of what we've accomplished."

"The bottom line," he said, "was that we came in and proclaimed that we were *going* to make it happen." As discouraging as it was to find the program in the shape it was in 1983, we immediately put out the word that Illinois was going to be very good. I'm not sure we always believed it, but that was our creed.

I had met Don when I was coaching at Pittsburgh. He telephoned me one day and said he'd just gotten out of the service, six years in the Air Force, and he was looking for a place to go to school and play volleyball. He had visited Penn State and wanted to visit Pitt. So I invited him to come to a practice, which was legal then.

The practice he came to was a disaster. I had told the team early in the session, "If you guys don't pull your act together and get this done the right way, you might as well just go home. You're just wasting your time and mine." They didn't get any better, and I called practice right in the middle, sending everybody home. Don was leaning our way already, since his family was in the Pittsburgh area, but he later told me that my dismissing my players that day was one of the factors that made him want to play for me. He was impressed that I would make a threat like that and actually follow through on it.

Don played for me on the men's team, and I could see from the start that he had a keen grasp of the game. I asked him to help me as a student assistant with the women's team, and he also began to help out with the junior women's club team. We were working very closely together in volleyball, and we were also becoming fast friends. When I left Pittsburgh, I told him that there would be a day when I would get a go- for-it type of job, and he would be the person I'd call to be my assistant coach. He went to Ohio State and I went to New Mexico, and we talked maybe two or three times in three years. But when I got the Illinois job, I called him, and he never hesitated.

I consider Don one of the most creative, intelligent, insightful guys I've ever been around. I have a tremendous amount of respect for his intellectual powers, and for his practical common sense, two qualities that don't always go hand-in-hand. He's the kind of guy I want around when I'm making important decisions. And he was the perfect guy to have with me at the start at Illinois.

From the time Don and I met at the airport, we established where this program was going, and in our first meeting with the athletes, we laid down a set of principles that were going to govern the program. Wins and losses weren't even on the list at that point. We were concerned with establishing how we would talk about Illinois, what phrases and words we were going to use to describe our program and how we were going to present ourselves. Everything we did was going to be linked to a philosophy that was going to lead to success in the future.

An integral part of that philosophy involved going out into the community. When a new coach hits town, there's a honeymoon period. All of the program chairs of the civic groups in town ask the new coach to come and speak about the team. That was true even for a sport that wasn't exactly a marquee attraction. I was eager to speak to as many groups as possible — Kiwanis, Rotary, Optimists, you name it — and I played up the humble status of my sport. Jim Turpin, the station manager at WDWS/WHMS, likes to tell about when I spoke to his Rotary group in 1983. As Jim recalls it, I walked into a group of 200 people and held up a ball. "This is a volleyball," I said. "You don't recognize it now, but you will in a very short time." Then I'd make my bold predictions about how exciting the community was going to find this sport and our team, and before long people around the community were saying, "Who is this brash guy?"

From Less Than Zero 95

The brashness was part of the plan: we wanted to make a bold entry into the Champaign-Urbana community and get people talking about Illini volleyball.

And we played the same game with the regional and national volleyball community and the press. Every time I got a chance to be interviewed by anybody, I would make more bold predictions, bordering on the ridiculous, about the future of Illinois volleyball. I remember telling Bill Feldman of Midwest Volleyball, "Within two years, Illinois will be challenging Purdue and Northwestern for the Big Ten championship." Don and I were out there saying virtually anything that would get the program attention.

I'm sure people were shaking their heads, saying, "Boy, are those guys digging a hole for themselves!" And you couldn't blame them. Illinois was the volleyball doormat of the state. Illinois State would beat up on us, Southern Illinois would kill us, Eastern Illinois beat us in my first year, Illinois-Chicago beat us. And Northwestern was the best of the bunch. There wasn't a Division I program in the state that hadn't grown accustomed to feasting on the Illini. So when I came in boasting that Illinois was going to be a nationally prominent program, it triggered several reactions. Some people were asking, "Who are these idiots?" Some people were resentful of our cockiness, rooting for us to fail. But some — the ones we were really targeting — had to be curious: "Are these guys for real?"

In September, just a month after my arrival, I set up an "Illinois Volleyball Coming-Out Symposium" in the Chicago area. An Illinois booster was running the Hilton in Lisle, and we sent out fliers to everyone involved with volleyball in the Chicago area. We invited everyone to come meet with me, Don Hardin, sports psychologist Dan Smith and Karol Kahrs. We announced that the UI program had gotten a budget boost and was ready to start competing with the big players in volleyball. It was a pivotal meeting. There wasn't a huge turnout, maybe 25 or 30 people, but *who* was there was more important than how many. Some were volleyball groupies, some were USVBA players, and there were some key people in our future, several recruits, including Disa Johnson. We had a slide show and we all spoke to these people for about two hours. We probably overdid it, but we wanted to make our case: we were turning the program around, and we were going to recruit Chicago.

We didn't just start at zero, we started below zero, in the red numbers. When I arrived, the Illinois program was very unpopular with the state high school coaches and junior club coaches. In my first season, I was thrown out of two gyms in the Chicago area. Coaches would actually come up to me and say, "Oh, you're the new coach at Illinois? You're not welcome in our gym." Again, I don't think it was John Blair's fault, but I think the expectations for the Illinois program had been very high, and the performance hadn't matched the expectations. People felt as though the state university had let them down in failing to provide a quality program. To high school and club coaches, Illinois volleyball was low-level and unorganized, not worth pushing kids toward.

So we had to win some converts among the high school coaches, and among the club coaches as well. The way volleyball is organized, junior club coaches are even more influential than high school coaches in the recruiting process. A player might spend seven or eight weeks a year with her high school program and six months with her junior club program. Then, too, junior club programs attract the best high school players, making them ideal places to focus recruiting. So while we'd never ignore the high school coaches, we really centered our efforts on making good contacts with the club coaches.

All the work we put into public relations in the first two to three years paid huge dividends, though there were times we weren't so sure. I remember one speaking engagement at a women's club, hauling in my TV monitor and VCR and highlight tape. Suddenly I found myself in front of a room full of elderly women, half of them knitting or crocheting throughout my presentation. As I was giving my speech, it occurred to me: this had been one of those situations where the program chairwoman hadn't been able to find a speaker for the group. "Oh, my, we're really at a loss — who can we get to speak?" And somebody else had heard about me: "Hey, get this volleyball guy — he'll speak to anybody."

So there I was, delivering my gung-ho message about our pioneering women athletes. "This is a women's organization," I emphasized. "You should get out there and support the team. This is a significant cultural phenomenon." And the hottest part of the discussion afterward concerned who was going to bake the chocolate chip cookies for the next meeting. They were really nice to me, but when I finished and looked at their faces, I could tell what they were thinking was, "What in the world are you talking about, young man?" I packed up and slipped quietly out of the room — I don't think anybody had noticed me come in, nobody had noticed what I had to say, and they certainly didn't notice when I left. I was totally out of my league. But that was what we were doing — we'd speak to anyone who asked.

When I agreed to take the Illinois job, I explained to Karol that for the first three years of the program, I would work on everything. I would coach the team, recruit the players, promote the team, sell tickets, build public relations. Whatever needed to be done to put a better product on the floor and to sell that product, I'd be responsible. But I said, "After three years, the team's going to be good enough that I can't carry that whole burden any more. I'll have to devote all my attention to the team, and you'll have to develop a staff to take care of the publicity, marketing and promotion of Illinois volleyball." And that is exactly what evolved.

I knew that in an environment where virtually nothing had been done for the program, I couldn't just walk in and say, "I'd like 30 percent of all your time." It was my responsibility to first prove we would be worth the promotion and event management people's time.

To a great extent, what we encountered at the start at Illinois was just a reflection of a sort of "second-class citizenship" for volleyball everywhere in the country outside of the West. Volleyball is in a curious position. In the early to mid-1970s, when Title IX forced athletic departments across the country to create budgets for women's sports, overnight there was a bunch of teams, but a very small pool of coaches. Programs would reach out and grab anyone they could — that's how I got into it, after all. A lot of people were coming into women's athletics without a history, without a lifetime of formulating thoughts on how this should be governed and run.

You also had directors of women's athletics, hundreds created overnight. These weren't people who had a lot of experience handling large budgets and establishing priorities on a large scale. Suddenly those were the very responsibilities being laid on them. The influential administrators of that period, either consciously or unconsciously, selected basketball as the flagship sport of women's athletics. One reason was that there was an easy model to copy in men's basketball. It was a sport women could play, and the structure of it only needed to be copied from what had already been done for men. It was easy for people to relate to — sports fans already understood basketball statistics, points per game, rebounds, assists. We had a media corps already attuned to what these words meant and how to watch a game. We had television and radio that didn't have to invent a way to cover that sport. For whatever reasons, basketball was anointed, without a test period.

It would have been interesting if they'd said, "Let's block out a 25-year period, during which we'll watch the trends and tendencies that develop with all women's sports. We'll experiment, and see what catches on and what doesn't." I think if that had happened — if equal resources had been expended for each sport on promotion, national marketing, lobbying on NCAA committees — volleyball would have emerged much more quickly than it has as one of the premier women's sports. I don't have anything against women's basketball, but a lot of women volleyball coaches are filled with resentment and bitterness and frustration over the unequal treatment.

Wherever it's been given a chance to grow, volleyball has flourished, both with fans and with the press. We see what's being done for women's basketball, and we just shake our heads. If only we had half that support, our sport would be over the top right now. Maybe we have a chip on our shoulder, but it's the result of years and years of knowing we have a really good product, equal to, if not better than, basketball as a team sport for women. I'm lucky at Illinois because the Athletic Department has been so supportive of our women's volleyball program. But, I share the concerns of coaches at other programs who are not so fortunate.

Culturally speaking, women are nurtured to cooperate, to emphasize teamwork, while men are acculturated to be more confrontational. Certainly volleyball has confrontation, but the ball has to be circulated around your side of the net, without interference from the other team, and each offensive sequence requires considerable teamwork. No one can do anything without the assistance of a teammate. It really is tailored to the way females are acculturated around the world.

So why does basketball have three scholarships for each starting position, and we have only two? Basketball gets 15

From Less Than Zero

scholarships, we have to fight to save 12. Who decreed that? It's a basic statement at the start: you're not as worthy as basketball. When budgets are handed out, basketball is perceived to have greater needs. Their recruiting budgets are larger, and the basketball team has to travel in style, sleep in comfort, eat in good restaurants.

Some people would say at this point, "Well, Coach, that's the way it always is in athletics — the men's tennis team isn't going to get what men's basketball gets." But what I'm talking about is two sports that started out on a par. There were no records of great crowds for women's basketball any more than there were for volleyball. Women's basketball was just anointed. Now, I've had a great situation at Illinois. Karol has never subscribed to the assumption that basketball automatically takes precedence over volleyball, and the athletic directors, from Neale Stoner to John Mackovic to Ron Guenther, have always been willing to let it happen for our program. But there are scores of volleyball coaches around the country who have never had that kind of support, and as a group, it's hard for us to understand why.

We had no event management in 1983. It was almost like being back at Pitt — we set up the chairs, swept the gym, set up the scorer's table. Karol helped out as our P.A. announcer, giving the lineups and announcing the scoring over Kenney's decrepit old speaker box. Otherwise, our staff did everything because nothing had been done in the past.

If anything, we had event anti-management. Not only did we have to take care of everything ourselves, we had to defend the meager resources we were allowed. One Friday, Don and I set up the gym and left to get ready for that night's Big Ten match. When we returned to Kenney for the match, we found that all the sideline chairs — what passed for "team benches" — were gone. We have a match in less than two hours, and there's not a single chair in Kenney Gym — nothing for the players to sit on, nothing for the coaches to sit on, nothing at the scorer's table — just plain nothing.

We called Stadium Maintenance in a panic and found out that the order had gone out to round up all Athletic Association chairs and deliver them to the stadium for Band Day at Saturday's football game. High schools bands from all over the state would be visiting, and so we were supposed to make do without team benches. The other team showed up, and we were all sitting on the floor. Ten minutes before the match started, a guy from the stadium showed up with about a dozen chairs.

That was how low we ranked. Someone had said, "Get all of the chairs." Someone else had driven over to Kenney Gym, seen the place obviously set up for a volleyball match, but he had his orders. Forget the volleyball match, they don't need chairs for volleyball; we don't want this high school clarinet player to have to sit on the turf. Today, we get the same treatment as any other sport, but a decade ago, we might as well have been playing outside.

Then again, in 1983, we hadn't paid our dues, we hadn't proved that we deserved to get the same respect as the other athletic programs. We didn't have a good team, and we weren't drawing crowds — 50 people in the stands was cause for celebration. But we were building. That first year saw the creation of the Networkers, the Fighting Illini volleyball support group.

I started the Networkers with a handful of names. We had eight, maybe 12 people at the first meeting in the Varsity Room following the 1983 season. Don Clegg made a film; Dottie Pash was there, the wife of former Illini golf coach Ladd Pash; Bob Ruelle, Bill and Doris Higgins, and Wally Hendricks were among the originals.

Then, as the Networkers grew, a group of engineering people got involved — Jim Bayne, Carl Larsen, Jim Seyler. Jim Bayne used to pop popcorn all day and bring it in to sell at our first concession stand — a table on the Kenney Gym floor. It was all very primitive, but we were starting something that had a chance to evolve into a vital support group for a successful program.

In the first off-season, I devised a marketing plan and set up our promotions. The plan centered around a tightly organized timeline, January to December, specific dates when things had to be done. Here's who does what on what day, and here's when they report the results.

We still weren't drawing many fans that second season. It was still family and friends and volleyball purists at the matches. Once in a while somebody would get lost walking across campus, and a few strays would wander in to the gym to see us play. You could almost hear people saying, "What's going on here? Do they play some kind of sport at Kenney?"

From Less Than Zero

One memorable night in '84, we had our first band. I had called Gary Smith from the Marching Illini and tried to get a band for our matches. Gary does an outstanding job with the Marching Illini, always has, but he made it clear that day that volleyball was not any higher on his list than it was on the lists of the all the other campus offices where we were trying to get things done. Gary was diplomatic, but the message was unmistakable: "Coach, we don't have the time or the inclination or the money." He was running the band on a shoestring already, and there was nothing in the budget that would cover a trip to Kenney Gym for a volleyball match.

We looked into some alternatives, thinking maybe we could get a high school band, but we didn't come up with anything concrete. Then one day a graduate assistant, Sandy Davin, who was helping us that year with administrative tasks, told us she'd found a band. Great. When we got to the match that night, sure enough, there was our "band" way up in the corner of the west balcony sat two guys in cut-up jeans and moth-eaten T-shirts. One of them had a drum, the other a bass guitar. And all night long, they played the theme from the "Addams Family," over and over. I think it may have been all they knew. Da-da-da-dum, BOOM-BOOM, all night long, at any time — it didn't matter if play was going on or we were in a timeout — da-da-da-dum, da-da-da-dum, da-da-da-dum, BOOM-BOOM.

You might think some of the fans — and remember, there were still only a handful of people in the gym, so everyone could hear the "band" clearly — you might think they'd have some fun with the sheer surrealism of it, but no, nobody was getting into it. They'd start playing again — da-da-da-dum — and people would crane their necks, looking quizzically up at these two isolated creatures up in the far corner. I'm not sure these two guys even knew the match was going on; they certainly didn't vary their performance according to the action. It finally got under Don's skin so much it was all I could do to keep him from going up and throwing them out of the gym, or maybe killing them. We'd never seen them before, and we've never seen them since, but after that night we didn't feel so bad about not having a band.

Kenney Gym's capacity in 1984 was about 1,200, but it was such a dirty, filthy place we were going to be hard-pressed to draw a third that many fans. I looked around Kenney and thought, "What a pigsty. I am embarrassed to bring fans and athletes into this gym." But what could we do, we were stuck with it. Then I looked at the railing around the balcony, and I said, "What if we had colorful banners all the way around to brighten things up?" It wasn't going to turn Kenney into a showplace, but at least it would make it less dreary. But we didn't have any money — how do we get banners up there?

And that's how the idea was hatched to "sell" matches. Dianne Ricketts was assigned to our program, and she went to work selling banner space for each match to local businesses — $200 per match, $350 for a weekend package, something like that. If we sold everything for the entire season, we would make about $3,000 for the program, a huge amount of money then. Dianne went out and sold every single match.

In return for a sponsorship, we would have a banner professionally made for each sponsor. A place on one end of the gym was reserved for the sponsor of that night's match. Afterward, the banner would be moved to make room for the next match sponsor, but each banner would stay up on the railing for the rest of the season. We charged a little more for early-season matches, since those banners would have longer exposure.

We also asked the sponsors to put ads in the campus and city newspapers. Besides the banner space, we'd give the sponsors free tickets and some kind of special treatment, like limo service to the match. These initial contacts with local merchants helped lay the base for our future success in the community. Promotions like the Blimpie's Serving Contest helped spur fan interest. And our ability to attract local sponsors sent a signal to the administration: volleyball could work, both on the court and in the stands.

Don's 1988 assessment was right: we would never have gotten off the ground if I hadn't just barged into everything from promotions to public relations, to internal organization, demanding that volleyball be taken seriously, delivering my gospel to every group I could. "I guarantee, I promise, if you come to one match, you'll come back." I said that dozens and dozens of times in front of hundreds and hundreds of people, having no idea inside whether it was true or not. I projected the image of the confident go-getter — brash, creative, a bit of a gambler — and that attracted a lot of attention.

We set ourselves up to either win big or lose big, and that's the secret to athletics. You have to take risks, and that's always been my style. You set yourself up, you establish your foundation and you keep maintaining it, making the program successful on the floor and fun to watch. Then it's just a matter of waiting for that spark of electricity that will galvanize interest and support. And if all the molecules get aligned properly on a given day, then you're ready to take off, you're ready to strike it rich. We were ready in 1985.

RECORD BREAKERS

That galvanizing moment that creates a successful athletic program—the timing is so unpredictable. It can happen in one year or in 10 years. Look at John Wooden. How long was it before he started to win with UCLA's basketball program? He lost lots of games early on and didn't win any NCAA games for a long time. Then they turned a corner and became the most successful college program ever, in any sport.

It's a principle of sport that often gets overlooked. Study the successful programs and you'll find that what the coaches and athletic departments did before the success was keep things ready. It takes an enormous amount of commitment and work, but if you're not prepared for that galvanizing moment, it can come and go unnoticed, and nothing will happen. Many a coach is good in the gym, knows how to handle athletes and get good performances out of them, but the program never reaches the elite level because the coach hasn't paid enough attention to establishing and maintaining the foundation.

In 1984, our goal was to win eight matches in the Big Ten. The year before, our first season, we'd gone 3-11 and finished in the cellar, so we were asking for a big jump in '84. We wound up going 18-15 overall and 6-7 in the conference, but we came within an eyelash of our eight wins, losing a couple of very close matches. Finishing over .500 overall was an important step. We still weren't very good, but we were clearly on our way up, and we were starting to get the people who would play a big role in later years.

The 1983 season had been characterized by a group of players without much talent who worked very hard and established the new message of our program, that Illinois was turning it around. That group carried itself very well all season long. We were reworking the philosophical underpinnings of the program, and we asked a lot of them. The natural tendency in a group that's been together for a while is to resist change, particularly if they're not seeing any immediate benefits from the change. When we didn't win right away, it would have been easy for that first group to give up on themselves and on us, but they stayed with us. I think they were willing to make sacrifices because they respected the coaching staff and appreciated what we were trying to do. I liked those players, they were good kids, but more than that I respected them for their willingness to buy into a new deal.

The 1984 team built on what the '83 group had done and made a statement of its own. Denise Fracaro was a junior, and Disa Johnson, Paula Douglass, Buff Binkley and Lori Anderson were freshmen. That freshmen group was the turnaround class. Disa came in and did a great job right away as our setter, and Lori was a coup because we had grabbed a quality recruit away from Mick Haley and his powerful Texas program. But the most important player in those years was Denise Fracaro.

Denise represented the transition from the old system to the new. And she'd resisted it at first, she hadn't been eager to buy into our new system. She was more comfortable doing things the old way in 1983. In 1984, she started to come around and was kind of on the fence about how we were doing things. But when she came back in '85, she came back as our captain and had a terrific season. She was our emotional and spiritual leader, and our performance leader on the floor. More than any other player, Denise embodied the transition of the Illini program from cellar-dweller to contender.

In 1985, Denise was the catalyst for our success. Mary Eggers was getting the headlines, our sensational freshman, but Denise was the emotional leader. Midway through that season, we had won 19 matches in what would become an incredible 30-match streak when we headed up to Minnesota. It came down to Game 5, and we were losing 10-2, the winning streak on the line. Worse than that, as far as Denise was concerned, we were getting beaten up at Minnesota again.

We took our second timeout and gathered around the bench. Denise came to the huddle and was absolutely possessed.

Record Breakers

I'll never forget her words: "I'm a senior this year and I am not losing to this team again," she said. "I am not leaving this building without beating Minnesota." And she made good on her vow, bringing us back for a 16-14 victory.

Eggers, Chris Schwarz, Disa Johnson, Sandy Scholtens and all the other new players played a big role in our success, but Denise was the toughest kid we had. She was the best blocker we have had at Illinois, and through determination and hard work, she turned herself into a great defensive player in the back row. Denise mirrored the program — starting at one level, and doing the work necessary to reach the next level, and then the next. If I were to choose one player to represent what happened in the early years at Illinois, it would be Denise Fracaro. Mary Eggers, just starting out when Denise's career was ending, would help take Illinois to an elite level, but without Denise, we couldn't have made the initial steps necessary to make the big step.

At the beginning of the season, we just wanted to be better than we'd been in '84. None of us had any idea what was about to happen, that lying ahead of us was a watershed season, marking the transition from a young and improving team to a nationally elite team. We had recruited Mary Eggers and Sandy Scholtens, and Chris Schwarz joined us as a walk-on, but nobody knew how good Mary was. I had watched her since her sophomore year, and she had always looked unorthodox. She was an Illinois kid, from West Aurora, and she played for Sports Performance, a good program to recruit from, but we really had no idea what we were getting.

At first, we weren't even sure we *were* getting her. When we were recruiting Mary, she was as quiet as a sphinx, rarely said a word. When you're a recruiter and you get silence on the phone and during home visits, you get the feeling that this recruit isn't very interested in what you have to say. Mary had narrowed her choices down to Western Michigan, Illinois State, and Illinois. Western Michigan was the power of the Midwest in 1984, drawing huge crowds and recruiting the best players from Sports Performance. Illinois State was the in-state power, a Top 10 team in 1984. ISU had always been seen as the place for female volleyball players to go if they were going to stay in Illinois.

Other schools had recruited Mary, but no one thought she would be a superstar. We were happy to get her, but we didn't think she'd be the one to elevate our program. At 5-10 1/2 or 5-

108 MIKE HEBERT: The Fire Still Burns

11, she was small for a middle blocker, even in those days. And she was so unorthodox, she just didn't jump out at you as a blue-chip recruit. But we recruited her and Sandy, a great ball control player. Chris, who became a really inspirational back-row player and backup setter, also joined us.

We added something besides players, too; we added a valuable experience. When I took the job at Illinois in 1983 I was assured that the athletic department would give its full support to our program. One thing I asked for and received was the athletic department's promise to fund a team trip to Europe. In the spring of 1985, we'd made our first trip to Europe, winning a tournament in Holland, and that trip would keep paying dividends throughout 1985 and '86. A spring or summer trip allows a team to come together as a unit, to learn how to work together in unfamiliar surroundings against unfamiliar competition. It is no accident that we have had a terrific season after every trip to Europe. The rules make it so difficult to get teams together to do things in the off-season. That's particularly important at the college level, to have that social interaction, to have some time together away from the gym, away from the training room, just to get to know one another.

There was one other experience about this time I'd just as soon forget, one that gave me my first insight into the petty side of some of my colleagues. Another coach went to the NCAA accusing me of three violations. According to the charges, we had made an improper offer of travel to the parents of a recruit; we had provided excess transportation — use of a limousine — to that recruit; and we had provided recruits with mementos of their paid visits.

That coach never called me, nobody from the coach's school ever called, the athletic director never got in touch to see whether there was some misunderstanding that could be re-solved. The coach just heard something and blew the whistle, either assuming I was guilty or not caring, just wanting to stir up trouble. Well, we figured out the basis for each of the accusations, and we weren't guilty of anything.

The first two had to do with a recruit we invited for a visit after I'd just come here from New Mexico, at a time when we were still getting used to the change-over from the AIAW to NCAA rules. I'd told the parents we could fly them out here, but when I called the NCAA to confirm that such a flight was permitted, I was told it wasn't. I immediately called the family and said, "I have egg on my face; I was wrong, I have to withdraw that offer." We never did anything wrong.

When the athlete made her visit, I told her we'd cover a limo from her home in Los Angeles to the L.A. airport. Now when most people in Champaign talk about a "limo," we're talking about a local transportation service, Corky's, that's basically a nice taxi, nothing fancy. But our attorney's investigation found that this athlete had taken it upon herself to take a $150 stretch limo, with a bar and a television, to the airport, charging us for it. It turned out later, after we hired an attorney to investigate, that that athlete had hired her boyfriend, who was a limo driver, and had given him a kickback. We were cleared of any wrongdoing.

The third charge arose because the Big Ten had sent out a memo saying the NCAA had made it legal to provide a small memento of a campus visit — a T-shirt, a cap, a sweat shirt, little things like that. It turned out that the Big Ten was wrong. The other two accusations were dropped altogether, but the NCAA said that even though the Big Ten had misled us on the mementos, we were still in violation. They told us if the athletes paid for their souvenirs, we'd be off the hook, so we had to go to Mary Eggers and Sandy Scholtens and a few other recruits and say, "Sorry, but we need some money from you."

After we received the Letter of Inquiry from the NCAA, we hired Mike Slive, a lawyer specializing in NCAA investigations. He came in and audited our program. He told Karol Kahrs and me that of all the programs he had ever audited, ours was the cleanest and the best organized. That was good to hear, but I was still devastated by the experience. I couldn't understand how somebody who didn't know me very well, who hadn't taken any time to investigate what might be an alternative explanation for our apparent misdeeds, could make those accusations without even talking to me first. Not only that, but the coach made it a point to talk to several people across the country, badmouthing me and my program. I really wasn't prepared for that. With the help of Mike Slive, we drafted a letter of response to the NCAA denying all allegations of wrongdoing and reporting on the findings of our own investigation. The NCAA took no further action and all charges against us were dropped.

I learned, though, that those things can happen in sports, and that a coach has little defense against that sort of accusation, public or private. Over the years, you hear a whole series of things about yourself and your program, rumors that make the rounds, most of them completely off the wall. You simply can't go around explaining, "By the way, we *didn't* do that." We'd get another painful lesson in that principle in 1992, when Dutch Olympian Kirsten Gleis came to play for us.

But we got everything cleared up, and we felt pretty good going into the '85 season. We won some early matches, including some exhibitions up in Chicago, and we felt even better. The first time we realized we were going to be really good was at the Las Vegas Invitational. We opened the tournament against Utah, coached by Julie Morgan, who's now at Illinois State. Julie is an excellent coach and her players always play hard for her. We gutted out a tough win over a good Utah team, 15-13, 15-13, 15-12, and then we beat Washington, another tough Western team. After both of those matches, I heard players walking off the floor talking about the embarrassment of losing to Illinois, this school from nowhere. "They're no good," I heard one player say. "We'll get them in the playoffs." The *playoffs?* Hey, we must be getting somewhere.

At the hotel that night, the father of one of the players from the University of California came up to me and started chatting about the tournament. Well, actually, he was chatting about his daughter and the Bears, who were ranked 12th in the nation at the time. He didn't mean to be condescending, I'm sure, but all he could talk about was how great Cal had played that day and how impressed we would be when we saw them and how fortunate we all were that a West Coast team of Cal's caliber had consented to travel all the way to Las Vegas for the tournament.

We beat San Diego and UNLV and faced Cal in the finals. We just thumped them, 15-9, 9-15, 15-9, 15-4. To that proud father's credit, he made a point of finding me again after the championship match. He shook my hand and said, "I'm really impressed with your team," and then just turned away. Well, I couldn't argue with him: *I* was beginning to be impressed with our team. Winning that tournament, against all that West Coast talent, was the high point to date of my first three seasons at Illinois.

The next weekend we went west again, to the Brigham Young Invitational, one of the nation's most prestigious tourna-

Record Breakers

ments. I had coached Pitt and New Mexico teams in the Invitational, and we had gone there in 1984 and lost four of seven matches. Winning the BYU tournament would brand a team as a legitimate power. We beat Eastern Washington to open the tournament, then gutted out another victory over Utah. And another win and another, and suddenly we've won our second Western tournament in two weeks.

Don and I were pinching ourselves. Was this really happening? We weren't doing anything differently, but we were winning every match. Don was doing a radio interview about this time, and the interviewer asked, "When you've won so many in a row, do you change anything?" and Don blurted out, "Naw, at this point I don't even change my underwear." But jokes and superstitions aside, it's true that when you're in a streak like that, it's not because you're doing anything differently. You coach the team, play the match, go back to the hotel, eat a meal, get up the next day. But some teams are 13-5 and some teams are 18-0, which is what we were, unusual terrain for Illinois. And we were doing it with style, we were tough, we were gutting out long, close games.

People were beginning to notice us, too, both nationally and on campus. At the beginning of the season, our crowds still hadn't been good, but when we came home from the two tournament championships, we started to notice a few more people in the stands. And then came the brainstorm.

Tom Boeh deserves most of the credit for the "Let's Break the Record" campaign. Tom was our promotions and publicity director, a real breath of fresh air, and his arrival goes a long way toward explaining the success of our program. His hiring illustrates a real gift of Karol Kahrs'. Here's a guy who walked into Karol's office without invitation and said, "I'm your guy." Karol gave him a hearing, liked what she heard and hired him. It wasn't a matter of having the right credentials but of having the right attitude. Karol took a chance, and her instincts were perfect.

Tom really had his finger on the pulse of the community. "Listen," he said, "the football team's struggling, and you guys are undefeated. Let's capitalize on it." He talked about some promotional ideas with Don and me, and the light went on when he discovered that Purdue held the record for attendance at a Big Ten match with something like 1,400. "Hey, we can beat that," he said. And he set the wheels in motion.

We were 21-0 heading into an October 4 date with Iowa at Kenney Gym. Everywhere Tom went, he talked about "The Streak." "Undefeated" became his favorite word, as he encouraged people to come out and be part of the record-breaking crowd he was promising for the Iowa match. He had the perfect touch, knowing just what to talk about and how to capture the excitement and focus interest. As Tom was quick to recognize, people like the idea of taking part in a record, and that "undefeated" piques their interest. I don't care if its croquet, somebody's going to say, "Undefeated? Nobody can beat 'em? Let's find out what that looks like."

So we went into that Iowa match shooting for win No. 22 but also with an eye to the attendance record. We had no clue how successful the promotion had been, and we went to Kenney Gym that night not knowing what to expect. There were two ticket takers, as always, no ushers, no parking attendants; nothing had been changed in anticipation of big waves of people. But you could tell, as the gym began to fill up early, that something was up. It wasn't just family and friends and the usual volleyball junkies; there were people in the stands we'd never seen before.

We expected the tide of fans to ease up as match time approached, but instead it kept increasing. People were coming from everywhere, and just when you thought the gym wouldn't hold any more, here came another wave. I looked outside at one point, and there were hundreds of people lined up waiting to get in, though the gym was already packed. The ticket takers were completely overwhelmed. After the match had started, I turned around on the bench and saw a guy trying to climb in through a window, being beaten back by a maintenance man with a broom. It was total and absolute chaos.

And that night, people discovered how intense Kenney Gym could get if you yelled. It was the first time Illinois ever had a big crowd for a volleyball match, and nobody knew what to do. There was no band, nothing organized, and the majority of the crowd didn't know the rules, didn't know how to cheer at a volleyball match. After a while, crowds get into habits, but nobody had any traditions to rely on; all they knew how to do was yell, and that worked just fine. The Illini cheerleaders had been practicing in the upper gym where our gymnastics teams practice, and when they heard the noise, they came down in street clothes and started leading cheers.

Our team thrived on the chaos. It was loud and hot, we were 21-0, and our players were confident and ready to play to the crowd. The Iowa team, on the other hand, was shaken up, unnerved, intimidated. No one had ever seen a crowd like this in the Big Ten. Sitting on the bench, everybody felt the same thing: this is special, we're into something tonight. Steve Kelly did a live remote for WCIA-TV, capturing some of that excitement. Mary Grady, who was working with our program that year, just walked around with a videotape machine, recording the scene. We knew we were making history. We played great, we won 3-0, and a whole new era of Illini volleyball was born that night.

The official attendance that night was 2,632, but there were more people there than that. In later years I began to get a feel for the size of the crowd at Kenney, when we were more organized and getting accurate counts, and that night against Iowa the crowd was bigger than reported. They were everywhere, standing all around the gym, and nobody was counting or regulating the crowd. The staff was caught way out of position. It was our first day of surfing, and we weren't ready for the size of these waves; we got chopped up pretty good by the undertow. This was something new and completely unanticipated that the administration was going to have to begin to deal with.

If the success of the "Let's Break the Record" promotion was beyond what anybody expected, the crowd the next night may have been an even bigger surprise. For Northwestern, without the big promotion, we drew 2,100. It wasn't just a one-shot deal — people came back. From that time on, we've drawn great crowds, 1,000 or more a night, after never having more than 700 before that. I don't think there's a program in the country that has outdrawn us over the last eight seasons.

A few nights later, on October 8, we played Purdue, the league leader and one of the dominant programs in the Midwest at the time. Purdue had won two Big Ten titles in a row and was clearly the best team in the league, led by All-American Marianne Smith. It was our most significant Big Ten match yet, and another big crowd at Kenney. On the very first play, the Boilermakers set Smith on the left side, and Mary Eggers went up and roofed her straight down. Mary went into her war dance around the net, the crowd went wild, and the match was over right then. We beat Purdue 3-0, a huge, huge victory, a pivotal match. All of a sudden, Purdue was knocked off the pedestal, and we were in first place, with the confidence that we could beat anyone in the Big Ten. Purdue was stunned. When you have been on top for so long, it is unnerving to get knocked off.

Denise, Mary, and Disa had made a statement: they didn't care about anybody's reputation; they were going to play you hard, and they were going to beat you. But afterward, our players were very subdued in the locker room, as though they were saying, "Well, sure we won — what did you expect?" There was no huge celebration, it was just a solid, satisfying victory. There were a few high fives, but mostly it was, "Let's get ready for next week."

What a magical season — the crowds, the early-season tournament wins, the streak, beating Purdue and Iowa. Now we were on the map, now we were nationally ranked. We're No. 20, we're No. 15, No. 13, No. 12, No. 8. By the first of November, we were 30-0 and everybody knew our name. We were in Chicago to play at Northwestern, and I got a call at our suburban hotel from WLS-TV. Mike Adamle sent a limo to bring me down to the studio on State Street. We did a long interview, the coach of the nothing team from nowhere talking about his team's 30-match winning streak. We'd come a long way from having to rope off our court for practice.

Then we went out and got beat, a tough 3-1 match. It was a legitimate loss — Northwestern played hard and deserved to win, but we just couldn't get the breaks or the calls all night, and we lost three close games, 15-13, 15-12 and 18-16. We could have won it, but we'd already won a couple of really close matches, we'd already been dealt our share of breaks.

The loss made the next night at Iowa the most important match to that point, a moment of truth for our players. Iowa had a couple of extra incentives to beat us. They were really embarrassed about how they'd played in front of our big crowd, and I'm sure they felt a little picked on, too — why were *they* the team that had to be there the night we broke the record? And we came in off our first loss, vulnerable.

We lost the first game 15-9, then turned it around and won the next two 15-12 and 15-5. In Game 4, we collapsed, falling behind 14-1. We're still drained from a tough loss the night before, and we're one point away from Game 5 against a fired-up team looking for a payback in its own court. Lose that one, and suddenly "The Streak" starts to mean something new. Once

Record Breakers

again, Denise Fracaro bailed us out, serving, blocking everything in sight, running around with her fist in the air, pumping everyone up. Before we knew it, we'd scored 15 consecutive points to steal a win, and we skipped out of Carver-Hawkeye Arena before anyone could take it back.

Three days later, we played at Purdue to decide the Big Ten title. The match was at Mackey Arena, the Boilermakers' basketball home, and Purdue got its attendance record back, drawing more than 4,000 fans. We were on the receiving end of the crowd noise this time, but unlike Iowa at our place, we kept our poise and played a great match. Unfortunately, so did Purdue, beating us 15-13 in the fifth game. Our players were devastated, but even though we hadn't won the Big Ten, our 31-2 record showed how far we'd come in three years.

We finished the regular season with seven more wins and got an at-large berth in the NCAA tournament, Illinois' first NCAA appearance. The selection committee didn't do us any favors, though: a No. 4 seed in the Mideast Region meant we drew top-seeded Western Michigan in the first round at Read Fieldhouse in Kalamazoo. We were cannon fodder. Not only was Western Michigan expected to go to the Final Four, the Broncos were *hosting* the Final Four. Some people were picking them to win the national championship, and they had the talent to do it. They weren't apt to let some upstart program spoil their party.

All the cards were stacked against us. Western Michigan was the power in the region, and it seemed likely to hold onto that status for a while. The Broncos had a terrific bunch of recruits, including some top Canadian players. Western Michigan had a great national reputation, as well: Rob Buck, a Chuck Erbe disciple, had been national Coach of the Year in 1983, and he was one of the rising stars in college coaching. This was the marquee program of the Midwest. They were pioneers at WMU — they had live radio, a band, and to top it off, the Broncos also led the nation in attendance.

The day before the match, Neale Stoner called my wife and said, "Sherry, why don't you get Kim Hardin and meet me out at Hangar 2. We're going to charter a plane, and I'm taking you and Kim up to Kalamazoo." He flew up with them, had the plane stocked with drinks for them, and he sat with them during the match. Don and I knew nothing about it, didn't even know they were there until after the match.

What a classy move. They were only gone for six, eight hours, because Sherry and Kim both had to be back at work in the morning, but what Neale did for us there was the kind of thing he did for a lot of people, and that's why a lot of people liked him. Illinois has done so many things for me over the years that have left me with a nice taste. Then of course winning is where it starts; they don't do that sort of thing if you're not winning.

Our first NCAA tournament appearance wasn't exactly a ride in style. When we showed up in Kalamazoo, no one really greeted us or took care of us. I had the feeling that the Western Michigan people were busy planning the Final Four, and this match was a formality that had to be endured to get to the regional and the Final Four. We weren't "Illinois" to them, we were just "First-Round Loser."

We changed in a classroom at Read Fieldhouse and hit the court, the upstarts from Illinois, the team with the loud, bold coach, and we won the first two games 15-9 and 15-11. Eggers was hitting and blocking and running around the gym, fist in the air, glaring through the net as if to say, "I don't care *who* you are, we're gonna thrash you." Our whole team played like that, making this statement in the first two games that we weren't afraid of Western Michigan, the Final Four, the 4,000 fans, the radio, the band or anything else.

Western came back and won the third game 15-12, and the night was still in doubt. Two things could have happened at that point. Western could gain the momentum and rally to win, or we could bounce back strong and regain control of the match. We won 15-2 — strong enough for you? Their crowd, their radio people, their coaches, their players, everybody was stunned. Sherry and Kim and Neale came down to congratulate us, and it was our turn to be stunned. To have won a match as big as this, and then to have our loved ones there to share it — perfect.

I'll never forget that scene. We literally ran from the court back to our classroom, fists in the air, giggling, just having a ball. Everything was deathly silence in the gym except for us. We had screwed up all of the great plans at Western. That was how 1985 went for us, one storybook after another. All season long, we were just not expected to be this good, we weren't supposed to be beating these teams. We were 39-2, and we were still surprising people.

On to Lincoln, Nebraska, to meet Chuck Erbe and USC. Southern Cal was on another level. We played reasonably well at times, but we lost 3-0. We had run the string as far as it was going to run that season. The match was our first on radio, broadcast on WDWS. Mary Grady, the volleyball coach for years at Glenbard South High School, was at Illinois on sabbatical, and she was the color analyst for the broadcast. Doing play-by-play was Mike Kelly, his first stab at volleyball. I remember sitting down with Mike explaining the sport to him, drawing diagrams of plays and situations. Mike did a good job on the match, making up for his incomplete knowledge of the game by conveying the enthusiasm. Mike's a big-time guy now at KMOX in St. Louis, but he cut his teeth broadcasting Illini volleyball.

Southern Cal ended our glorious season, but we had accomplished more than we could have hoped for. We went 39-3 and turned everyone in Champaign-Urbana on to volleyball. Suddenly we could go anywhere to recruit without having to convince people we were a legitimate team. I had no more doubts about whether volleyball would work at Illinois. I could call friends now in the coaching business and get on the schedules of top teams. San Jose State, the nation's top-ranked team, was going to come to our Illini Classic. We were invited to play in the inaugural Mid-America Classic in Chicago, now the Reebok Challenge run by Bill Feldman. Western Michigan was coming to our place. We had joined the elite.

VICTORY CIGARS

My first home match at Illinois in 1983 was a 3-1 loss to Western Michigan. From then on, starting with that huge defeat in the '85 playoffs, I don't know what it is, but Illinois just can't lose to the Broncos. Many of the matches have been extremely close, including the most difficult match I have ever coached, a 3-2 NCAA regional win in 1987, but they could not get over the hump on us. I don't know if Rob Buck would agree, but I think we've been one of the biggest reasons for Western Michigan's relative decline in the Mideast Region.

It's been a great rivalry. I don't care what players were on the court, anybody in an Illinois uniform knew the history of the rivalry, and no team wanted to be the one to lose to Western Michigan. We'd be down 2-1 and come back to win in five. At Kenney, at Read, it didn't matter. They always had a great team, and I have a lot of respect for Rob Buck's coaching ability, but somehow we'd always find a way to win. I can't explain it, but dominating the series was a significant statement for us to make in the region, that the status WMU had held was now ours.

After the success of 1985, we ran off three straight Big Ten championships, losing just one conference match in that span. In 1986, we brought in two outstanding recruits, middle blocker Nancy Brookhart and outside hitter Bridget Boyle. Denise Fracaro was gone, but adding Brookhart and Boyle to a solid nucleus of Johnson, Scholtens and Eggers gave us a good team that figured to stay good for a few years.

In '86, we knew we had a good team, but we just didn't know how good. Goal setting has always been one of my talents, getting a feel for a team, for its personality, and structuring goals to meet that team and its skills. But for some reason, I was finding it hard to articulate a goal for this team. We had just missed out on the Big Ten title in 1985, and I knew we were good enough to win it. I'd been making bold predictions for three years, but now that I had a really good team, I found myself waffling, unwilling to go out on a limb. It was totally out of character for me.

Don and I hashed things over before a team meeting. How were we going to word it, what would our goal be? I asked Don, "Do we tell the team we've *got* to win the Big Ten, do we say we're *going* to win the Big Ten, do we say we *could* win the Big Ten? What do we say?"

Suddenly Don had an inspiration. He looked at me and said, "Here's what we do: not only are we going to win the Big Ten, but we're going to predict *how* we're going to win it. We are going to *clinch* the Big Ten championship on November 19, at home against Purdue."

"You're crazy," I said, but the more I thought about it, the more I realized what a brilliant piece of goal-setting Don had come up with. I bought into it, and so did the team. We wouldn't publicize it, but with our team, all year long, it was, "We are going to clinch against Purdue." The word "clinch" was critical — not "We're going to try to beat Purdue," not "We're going to hope to play as well as we can and maybe sneak a win," but "We're going to *clinch* the championship" against Purdue, the defending champion, our archrival in the Big Ten, and, to this point, our nemesis.

Don's approach was perfect because it preempted any doubt that might ever creep in, it banned any halfway thinking. It changed the entire psychological atmosphere of our program that year. Just one thought: Clinch . . . against Purdue. Why not? Choose the toughest opponent. Use the word "clinch," forcing the team into a completely confident wipe-out philosophy. And say we're going to do it at home in front of our fans. We'd wrapped everything up in one package.

Sure enough, November 19 came around and we were undefeated and in first place, one game ahead of Purdue. If we win, it's a clincher. Another big crowd, of course, including Lou Henson, the men's basketball coach, and Mike White, the football coach. It was the first shot for a Big Ten championship by an Illinois women's team. Bev Mackes' gymnastics team had won a title a few years before, but that was before the Big Ten had

Victory Cigars 121

sanctioned women's play, and it was just an unofficial collection of Big Ten teams. This was official.

It was a really weird match, but victory seemed inevitable. We played sloppily, we couldn't serve, couldn't do anything right, but it didn't matter — we knew we were going to win. We hadn't left ourselves any choice. We lost the first game 16-14 but won the last three 15-9, 15-4, 16-14. The Networkers had already bought a 1986 Big Ten Championship banner, and the minute the last point was scored, the banner was unfurled on the east balcony. It was a milestone for Illinois women's sports.

The conference championship was not only the highlight of the season, it was the foundation on which everything was built that year. Before the Big Ten matches started, we'd started a little slowly, winning the Florida Invitational but losing the Illini Classic title to top-ranked San Jose State in front of a big Kenney crowd. The next weekend we played in the Mid-America Classic, losing the title to Nebraska 3-1. We were still ranked, still playing well, but we weren't winning the huge matches. Nebraska and San Jose State were Top 10 teams, and we weren't, at least not yet.

We beat Western Michigan 3-1, then started the conference season. We had built momentum with 16 Big Ten wins by the time we went down to San Marcos and played Southwest Texas State late in the year. Early in the match, Bridget Boyle went down with a hyperextended shoulder and was out of the match. Nancy Brookhart was already nursing an infection in her knee, and though we didn't know it at the time, she had come down with mononucleosis as well. We beat Southwest Texas State, then went to Austin the next night to play sixth-ranked Texas. Somehow we beat the Lady Longhorns 3-2, winning the fifth game 15-6. We won our last two Big Ten matches, and suddenly a team that hadn't been winning the big matches early on had closed with two tough road victories and the cappers to a perfect conference season. But we learned going into the playoffs that Brookhart and Boyle, our heralded freshman starters, were finished for the year.

We got a first-round tournament game at Kenney Gym, beat Northern Illinois 3-1 after losing the first game, then headed to Lincoln to face Western Michigan in the regional semifinals. Don Hardin developed a great game plan to compensate for our two missing starters, and we practiced really well and just thrashed Western Michigan, 15-5, 15-10, 15-4. Buff Binkley blocked in the middle for us that night. She had no business blocking in the middle at that level, but we gave her a game plan, and she followed it to perfection. We said we want you to commit on this person at this time at this place—just jump, and they'll set it right there. We were just guessing, but we guessed right. Buff had 12 blocks that night, and her early blocking was one of the main reasons we won. Western was used to running certain plays that just inevitably resulted in kills, had all season long. We screwed up their plan by guessing on the blocking commits and got them frustrated early.

The next night, we were hammered by Nebraska in the regional final, 15-9, 15-8, 15-3. The Cornhuskers went on to finish second in the NCAA tournament, while we, despite losing two key players down the stretch, had gone one step beyond the year before.

Heading into 1987, we knew we had the best middle-blocking tandem in America in Mary Eggers and Nancy Brookhart. Many teams had one great middle blocker, but who had two like ours? They gave us the nucleus for a great team, and with setter Disa Johnson, now a senior, we had depth and experience as well. And we continued to bring in top recruits. We beat UCLA and Stanford to get Laura Bush, a central Illinois product from Strasburg, and we also landed Lisa Dillman and Barb Winsett. Our goal was to repeat as Big Ten champion and to go one more step in the NCAA tournament, to win the regional title. We had a lot of cards on the table. And we had cigars on our desks, too.

In February, I'd gone to Cuba with the U.S. national team. On our way out of the country, I bought two Romeo y Juliet cigars in fancy aluminum containers, one for me and one for Don. Back in Champaign, I gave Don his cigar. "Don," I said, "when we win the regional championship, we're going to march right into the locker room, and we're going to light up these big Cuban cigars in front of our team, and we're going to celebrate." I told Don to keep his cigar in plain sight on his desk. I kept mine in the pencil cup on my desk from February until the end of the season.

Every time I looked at the cigar, spring, summer and fall, it was a reminder of our goal: the regional championship. I thought about that cigar a lot, and it really motivated me. We didn't tell the team. Like the Big Ten clincher the year before had been a private motivator for the team, the cigars were a private symbol between Don and me.

Victory Cigars

The '87 season started with a 3-1 victory over Oregon, the first Pac-10 team ever to visit Kenney Gym. We beat Arizona State and Texas A&M in our Illini Classic, but lost to Brigham Young in the final, a legitimate loss to a very good team. Next we headed up to Chicago for the Mid-America Classic.

The rest of the field made this a very significant tournament for us. We opened with a victory over Illinois State, getting the in-state monkey off of our back. Then we beat USC and Chuck Erbe the next night, 15-7, 15-7, 15-7. In front of all of the Chicago recruits and on cable television, it was a huge win for us. For me personally, it was a victory over a program that had won four national championships, over a coach who is a volleyball legend and who had given me my first World University Games assignment six years earlier.

A week later, we went from those giddy victories to one of the most sobering losses I have had at Illinois. Kentucky came into Kenney Gym on a Sunday afternoon. It was Kathy DeBoer's first season, and I had agreed to play Kentucky to help out her program. The best way to improve a program that's starting out or that has fallen on hard times is to play top programs. Other coaches have helped me out that way when I was trying to get programs established, so I've always tried to do the same.

We had an open weekend except for this match. I didn't want to play on Sunday afternoon, but we had to because of the Wildcats' schedule. So we went out and lost in five games. We almost came back to win after trailing 13-4 in Game 5, but Kentucky held on, 15-13. The victory catapulted Kentucky into the Top 10, where they stayed for the rest of the season. The loss kicked us out of the Top 10.

I look back at Kentucky as one of the really frustrating losses in my career at Illinois. We were clearly the better team, but we got beat. A year or two later some of the players told me the team had taken advantage of its first in-season Friday-Saturday off in years by partying all weekend. They never took Kentucky seriously and just weren't prepared for the match. I failed to anticipate that, and we paid the price.

We opened the Big Ten by beating Purdue, so we were right on track there. We headed to Nebraska for a tournament, beating Tennessee and Loyola Marymount, then losing to Nebraska 3-2 in the feature match. That loss did more to focus our team and our staff than anything else we did in a two-year period. We expected to win the match, and we played well enough to win, but we didn't win. It was very frustrating because we were playing a little bit better than Nebraska overall, but we just couldn't win the right points. No sour grapes, that's just something that happens. Jay Potter was an assistant at Nebraska at the time and he recalls that on the bench, he and head coach Terry Pettit had no more idea why they were winning than we did. "Gee," they'd say, "Illinois is outplaying us in every phase of the game, but we've got a chance to steal the match."

We lost the fifth game 15-8, and our whole program was devastated. Back at the hotel in Lincoln, the postgame meal, the trip home, people were just despondent. We knew we had to beat the Cornhuskers to win the regional championship. We weren't playing badly, but in the space of two weeks, we'd lost to BYU, we'd lost to Kentucky, now we'd lost to Nebraska. It's not like we were getting kicked around — we'd lost one four-game match and two five-game matches — but we needed to find a way to turn those close matches around.

Once again, Don Hardin came to the rescue. While I was moping around, hanging my head, feeling sorry for myself, Don walked into my office and said, "Look, here's what we do: we dedicate every moment from now until the regional championship to the job of beating Nebraska. Every day, we'll do something in practice to prepare for that match. We'll watch tape, we'll meet every day. We will be obsessed with beating Nebraska in a regional final."

Don has a great gift for putting a twist on things, turning a negative moment into something positive. I've learned a lot from Don, particularly from the way he uses words and phrases to create a mood, the right atmosphere. Don's idea was to use the Nebraska loss as a springboard to a higher level of confidence, and that's what we did. Don had defined the previous season with the "clinch," and now he was giving us a target for 1987.

It worked. We memorized the Nebraska team, we looked at that tape over and over, worked on beating Nebraska each and every day. In practice we'd "link up" everything with our feedback: "You know, the reason I'm telling you this is that we're going to see Nebraska in the regional final, and to beat Nebraska we've got to know how to do this, and do it well. That's why I'm telling you this now. Sure, we're playing the last-place team in the Big Ten tomorrow night. That's not why I'm telling you this — we'll probably beat them. But we're going to do this right because we're going to beat Nebraska."

Everything was pointing to Nebraska, but we got a bonus out of our plan: by creating that tight focus, "Nebraska" made us better in our Big Ten matches. Then after winning 17 consecutive conference matches, we headed to the Wendy's Classic at the University of Pacific, where everything started to fall apart.

Only the elite teams are invited to the Classic, and it means big crowds, *Volleyball Monthly* coverage and television. There we were with Pacific, Texas, and UCLA. For me, getting into the Wendy's Classic was the result of years of networking and building the program and establishing credibility. John Dunning had finally invited us to the showcase tourney for the sport.

We played Pacific the first night and lost in four games, but I was pleased with the loss. We had played well and lost a close match to the two-time defending NCAA national champions on their own floor. The next night, we played Texas. Texas and Illinois were both ranked in the Top 10, and here was another showcase match for our program: big crowd, great arena, electric atmosphere, another big opportunity to show the nation that Illinois was for real. We went out and lost 15-4 in the first game and wound up losing the match in four games. I was devastated by our performance, really crushed, because I thought we had a better team than Texas. Here we were, ranked among the nation's top teams, undefeated in the Big Ten, playing the best teams in the West and South, and we'd lost two straight matches. We had missed an opportunity to make an important statement: Midwest versus West Coast, Midwest versus South. It was crucial to show we were better than Texas, and we hadn't done it.

Now we'd lost two in a row. We got back late Sunday night from a very long road trip, and we had to regroup for a match at Purdue two days later. We had already clinched the Big Ten championship, but we still had something to prove at Purdue. What we proved was that we could be horrible. We led 2-1, but lost the last two games 15-12, 15-12. I was just bananas now. Here we were, the Big Ten champions, and we'd lost three straight matches with the NCAA tournament around the corner. Everyone — the coaching staff included — was wondering what had happened to the Illini.

As is my habit after tough losses, I was circling the wagons at this point, giving very short, terse answers in interviews. I was looking inward trying to find the solution. The confident coach was missing in action. And now, to close the regular season, we had to host the same Texas team that had just beaten us in the Wendy's Classic. What happens if our team, which had seemed to be one of the best in the nation, went out there and lost a fourth straight match? What would that do to their confidence going into the tournament?

I hit on a surefire way of keeping that from happening. That team wouldn't even *play*. I declared it "Senior Night" and started all of the seniors. Buff Binkley had been replaced by Barb Winsett as right-side hitter, but she'd play this match. Disa Johnson had been playing, but Barb had been replacing her as a setter on occasion; not tonight. Lori Anderson had been replaced by Bridget Boyle, and Paula Douglass had never been a starter. I started Lori and Paula as my left-side hitters, Buff on the right side, Disa setting. I milked it with the press, announcing it was "Senior Night," a way of recognizing these players' contributions throughout their four years here. Well, it *was* that, but it was a strategic ploy, too.

I planned to play the seniors the whole match. I was determined not to come in with the regular starters, because that would send a message to the team that I didn't trust the seniors. It was a gamble, but as I saw it, there were three possible outcomes. One, the seniors come out and get thrashed, not what you want to see, but not as bad as having our core group lose its fourth straight. Two, it's a close match and we lose, or it's a close match and we win. Either way, the seniors have proved themselves, and the regular starters are still shielded. Three, the seniors pull off a miracle and win the match in convincing style. Obviously, that was the best option possible — not only do our starters get some rest and some inspiration, but our seniors pick up a surge of confidence. That result, unlikely as it might be, would really bring our team closer together and send them into the playoffs on a high.

And the miracle happened. Texas came into Kenney Gym and we beat them 3-0 with the seniors playing the whole match. Bridget Boyle never played a minute, Barb Winsett took the night off, we just benched everybody. Texas was getting ready for the tournament, too, of course, and maybe they didn't want to expend a lot of energy and effort, but it was a great win for us regardless. We broke a three-match losing streak and beat a Top 10 team in convincing style without our usual lineup. We headed into the tournament feeling good about ourselves. Our gamble had paid off.

Victory Cigars

We beat a really good Pittsburgh team 3-1 in the first round of the NCAA tournament, and here came Western Michigan again. What a donnybrook at Kenney Gym, the most gut-wrenching match I have ever been involved in as a player or coach. It was a great match technically, but it went way beyond that. It had a warlike quality. There wasn't a casual moment in the match. Every rally, every point, both teams were playing as hard as they could. From the very first serve to the last point, it was a bloodletting, every moment of it.

When it was over, the players were completely spent, the crowd was spent, the coaches, the officials — there wasn't a person in the gym who wasn't absolutely drained. Even the press, the guys who are supposed to be detached and objective, felt it. Joe Millas of the Champaign *News-Gazette* wrote a column about the match the next day, a moving column. He called it the most intense athletic contest he had ever experienced in his life. You could tell Joe wrote that from the gut, and a lot of people shared his feelings.

It was so difficult to score points in that match. It was a like a heavyweight bout, two sluggers standing toe to toe, neither one giving an inch. Both teams were on their game, and the crowd was insane, living and dying with every point. The noise level was as high as you can imagine. The gym was literally shaking, you couldn't hear anything. And it was like that for three hours, solid.

We were down 10-4 in the fifth game, and it looked like our bid for a championship was gone. My team was giving everything it had, but Western Michigan was just playing too well. I sat on the bench, completely out of moves. When I called my second timeout, I looked at Mary, Nancy, Disa, and there was nothing I could tell them. No point trying to motivate them — they *knew* they had to give everything, and they *were* giving everything. Now it just came down to the breaks of the game. All I said was, "Look, whatever happens, I'm really proud of you. I know you're playing your hearts out. Let's try to think about it one point at a time, just chip away. Don't get caught up in the winning and losing of the match, just stay in each point." Here and now, play the moment.

And that's how we won it, moment to moment, one painstaking point at a time. We scored the last 11 points, but it wasn't a "run" in the conventional sense, where momentum builds from one point to the next, the fourth point making the fifth point a little easier, the fifth paving the way to the sixth. No, every point was an ordeal, an emotional drain. Sideout, sideout, sideout, a long rally, another sideout. Finally we'd score a point, and it was like the whole gym would exhale in relief, even the Western Michigan people, because *something had finally been determined*, and you knew where you were again, and you could approach the match from that new level. And we'd say, "We only scored one point? It's taken us 10 minutes." So we'd gear up for the next one. One point at a time, we just dragged back.

At the end of the match, it was like nothing I'd ever experienced before. We'd made a miraculous comeback to win a magnificent match, we were going to play Nebraska for a spot in the Final Four, but instead of the hysteria you would expect from the Kenney Gym faithful, it was almost silent. A weary, bizarre silence, punctuated only by some polite applause. The crowd was so completely drained, no one had anything left to give. Then again, no one had to say anything—everyone knew what we had all just shared. It was like they had witnessed a gang fight. People filed out of the gym, speaking in low tones if at all. Several people told me later they didn't come back the next night for the regional final against Nebraska because they just couldn't handle another match. It's true that the crowd the next night was somewhat smaller.

At the press conference, Rob Buck and I met in the hallway, and we just stopped and looked at each other. We didn't exchange any words, we both just stared and shook our heads. And I think he realized that, while he'd have traded places with me in a second, I had the tougher task ahead. His players were going to have a hard time getting over that match, but mine were going to drag out of the gym at maybe 1 o'clock Saturday morning, then have to come back Saturday night to play the Cornhuskers, seeded No. 1 in the region.

One problem we didn't have, of course, was having to work out a plan to beat Nebraska — we'd been doing that all season long. All we did Saturday was remind the players, "Now it's time to do what we've been talking about the last two months." And the team came out like surgeons and just cut up Nebraska, 3-0.

One of my most memorable moments in all of volleyball, my whole career, came during that third game. I was on the bench, so absorbed in the match I hadn't even registered the

Victory Cigars 129

score. I looked up at the west scoreboard, and we were ahead 12-5, and for the first time it hit me: "Twelve-five? We're gonna win!" A whole range of emotions cascaded down on me. It was a moment of catharsis, like an out-of-body experience. All the planning, the program building, all the struggle throughout my career to get a team to this level, all the rash claims, the bold predictions — the feeling only lasted a moment, but in that moment I knew we were *there.*

The steamroller was in gear. We knew we were going to win, Nebraska knew it was all over. The crowd was chanting, "Final Four, Final Four," over and over and over, an exuberant contrast to the previous night's tension. I've always maintained that the real emotion in the NCAA tournaments, basketball as well as volleyball, comes in the regionals. I think the semifinals and finals of the regionals are the toughest competition, the biggest hurdles to get over physically and emotionally. Once you get to the Final Four, the hoopla takes over. You've already made it, you're among the elite — everybody is a winner at the Final Four. Friday night's match had tugged on every emotion; now, on Saturday, it was a release. Everyone was going bonkers, all hell had broken loose. Sherry ran across the floor to hug me, and it seemed like everyone was hugging and celebrating.

We took the players into the locker room for our post-game meeting. Before the match, I'd asked Don, "Do you have your cigar?" "It's in my pocket," he said. That was our first conversation about the cigars since I'd brought them back, but we'd been looking at them all year. So now Don and I pulled out our beautifully packaged Romeo y Juliets and lit them up. Neither of us smokes anything, so naturally we started hacking and choking after one puff. We were turning green, and the players were griping about all the smoke, so we snuffed our cigars after just that one puff. But the symbolism was there, anyway.

Then it was on to the Final Four in Indianapolis, a semifinal match against the No. 1 team in the country, Hawaii. I found out later that no one else gave us much of a chance. There were bets going around on how many points we might score in the match against Hawaii — the over/under seemed to be between 10 and 15. But just two weeks after falling on our faces at the Wendy's Classic and then losing to Purdue, we were playing as well as we had all year, and we weren't afraid of anybody. We knew we could win.

Well, I still know we could win, I still think we *did* win, but the record books don't back me up. We didn't get a single break in the match. I look back at the tape and see three separate times we won Game 1. Twice at game point — 14-6 and 14-10 — the linesmen didn't call Hawaii touches on balls Mary Eggers hit out of bounds off the block. A third call, game point again, Hawaii hit a ball out of bounds that was called in. We knew it at the time, the players knew it, and the tape leaves no doubt. Those things happen in sports, and I'm not blaming anybody, but had we gotten just one break, had we gotten the right call on any of those three plays, we'd have won Game 1. Instead, playing our butts off, we lost 19-17 to the No. 1 team in the country.

How frustrating. We were outplaying the nation's top-ranked team in the Final Four. We were showing the nation that Illinois can play ball, that we have a damned good team. But we just couldn't catch a break. I see that happen all the time in sports. The favored team, the coach with the reputation, the player with the reputation will always get the benefit of the doubt on the close call. It's not anything conscious or intentional on the officials' part, but they're human, and they're affected by reputation just like anyone else. Michael Jordan runs down the lane, bulls his way inside, he gets the basket and a free throw. Vinny Del Negro tries it, it's a travel or a charge. The call may have less to do with what actually happened than with who did it.

I think when a Hawaii player hits a ball off the block, the officials' eyes are trained a little harder on that possible touch than with the upstart team making the same play. I'm not saying that our program has been screwed over, I'm just saying that this dynamic exists in sports — the heavyweight champ is going to win the bout unless he gets knocked out. In fact, I see our program benefiting from the same principle now. Now we're the nationally elite program, and developing teams come into Huff Hall to play us, and I think we get the close calls. It's never intentional, it's just woven into the fabric of sport. A smart coach and a smart player will go into a match expecting that.

The same thing that killed us in the first game happened again in the second. We led throughout the game, but we couldn't get a break at the end and lost 15-13. We lost the third game 15-12, more of the same. Bridget Boyle hit a ball down the line and the linesman said she hit the antenna. Chris Marlowe, calling the match for ESPN, said the ball wasn't anywhere near the antenna.

We looked at the videotape and the ball was eight inches inside the antenna. What had happened was that it hit the tape of the net and jiggled the antenna. A routine call, but it turned into a violation on us.

It went down as a 3-0 loss, but we had played them much closer than that. Everyone who watched the match knew we had played well enough to win. Even Dave Shoji, the Hawaii coach, said we could just as easily have won. As far as we were concerned, we *had* won — and if they wouldn't let us play for the national championship, as least they had to admit we had established ourselves as a legitimate program that could play with anyone in the country.

ORBITING IN OHIO

The volleyball establishment started admitting we could play, all right: heading into the 1988 season, *Volleyball Monthly* picked Illinois as the No. 1 team in the country. That pioneering class was gone — Disa Johnson, Lori Anderson, Paula Douglass, Buff Binkley, the kids who embodied the program's turnaround — but an excellent team remained: seniors Eggers, Scholtens and Chris Schwarz, juniors Brookhart and Boyle and a sophomore class of Winsett, Bush and Dillman. But there were a few things *Volleyball Monthly* didn't know; heck, it took me a while to figure them out myself.

We made another trip to Europe over spring break in 1988, but this group was different from the '85 team. I had named Mary Eggers captain. She was a take-charge player on the floor, but she wasn't really ready for the off-the-floor responsibilities. I didn't feel anyone else was a better candidate, so I gave her the job. But during the trip, there wasn't any real leadership on the team, no one standing up for doing things the right way. It was a good group of people, but you need somebody to take charge, the way Disa Johnson could, the way Denise Fracaro could. Mary was the most splendid competitor I have ever coached, but I made a mistake in putting her in a leadership position that didn't fit her personality.

As a result, the '88 group didn't respond the way the '85 team had, and the European trip was a letdown for me. We played well and we did a lot of fun things, but that magical camaraderie wasn't there. The younger players didn't seem to want to be in Europe. They'd rather be back home with their friends. That reaction surprised me, and it tipped me off that this team was going to approach things in a different way. They played well and performed, which was the bottom line, but the chemistry was something strange to me, something I had to learn how to manage.

Something else I had to learn that year was to anticipate the dynamics of a coaching staff. Don Hardin had spent five seasons with me at Illinois, and he was such a quality person and a quality coach that I didn't anticipate what was about to happen. Don had been handling virtually all of our recruiting, but now he was starting to get pumped up about making a career for himself as a head coach. That made perfect sense — it was time for Don to move on to a head coaching job; he's extremely gifted, and he's proving that now at Louisville. And when Don left, I was really fortunate to hire Jay Potter at the last second. Sue Potter had already accepted a faculty position at Illinois, and Jay left Nebraska to join our staff. It was a good break for us.

The problem wasn't that Don had left — he's one of my closest friends, and I was thrilled to see him get that opportunity. The problem was that I failed to see it coming, and by the time I figured it out, most of the recruiting had been done. With the Louisville job looming, Don hadn't had his heart in recruiting the way he had in the past, and I didn't get involved until it was too late. As a result, we signed some kids we probably shouldn't have signed. One recruit showed up for three practices, then called her parents and went home. We'd never had that happen before. A couple of other players eventually transferred to get more playing time. The '88 recruiting group was our "lost class." These were all nice kids, but the class wasn't assembled with the painstaking attention to detail previous recruiting classes had received.

Petra Laverman also joined us that year from Jan Brugman College in Holland. The team didn't do a very good job of welcoming someone from a different culture to our team, certainly not like the old group would have. Petra's a pretty tough person to get to know, but I could tell by the way the team handled her arrival that everything wasn't exactly right.

Then there was one other problem we were about to discover. Barb Winsett had hurt her knee in the Final Four in Indianapolis. The damage was pretty severe, and she'd undergone off-season surgery, but she wasn't coming back well. She

Orbiting in Ohio 135

worked hard, did everything she could, but the knee wasn't responding. Her knee continued to deteriorate from then on, and it shook her confidence somewhat. Her mobility and jumping ability were reduced, and that knee injury held Barb back from becoming a really terrific player. She was a great kid, and a very good, sound player for us as it was. She made All-Big Ten twice, so she obviously had enough talent to play well despite the injury. But it was a shame the injury kept her from being the setter she might have been.

So here we were, the top-ranked team in the nation, heading to the Wahine Classic to face Hawaii, Pepperdine, and UCLA without a healthy setter. We opened by losing 3-2 to UCLA in a typical opening match: neither team played well, but we were supposed to win, and we didn't. The next night, we beat Pepperdine, but it was a shaky win. We closed the tournament with a 3-0 loss to Hawaii and limped home with a lot of questions about ourselves. No. 1 in the nation? Lots of other people were asking questions, too.

Barb's injury really defined our season. She was never really comfortable all season long. People think of an injury as something that keeps you out of the lineup until it heals, something that runs its course and then goes away, leaving the athlete as good as new. But some injuries are never going to go away, they're always getting in the way of the athlete's playing the game the way she once was capable of playing it. You can't play correctly, you can't even practice correctly — and not being able to practice right just pulls the level of your play down another notch. You start to question yourself — can you even go out and do your job any more? And on top of that it just plain hurts.

Barb had to deal with terrible pain, and she showed a tremendous amount of courage. She was getting a needle jabbed into her knee every other week to drain fluid. She would have it drained right before matches and then have to play on it. She was our setter, we had to have her. Behind Barb were Chris Schwarz and Martha Firnhaber. Without Barb, we were not a top-ranked team.

Even with Barb's shaky health, we went 18-0 in the Big Ten again. Unlike '86, it wasn't the result of any special plan or terrific inspirational effort. It was just a machine-like approach to beating teams. We simply had much more talent. We knew we were a good team, a veteran team with strong junior and senior classes. The '88 team didn't have the emotion and inspiration of the '86 and '87 teams, it just methodically went out and won with its rich supply of talent. The conference season was just something they had to get out of the way before the NCAA tournament.

We opened the tournament by beating Illinois State, then hosted the regional. We played Notre Dame, which had Julie Bremner at setter and Kathy Cunningham opposite her on the right side, and, won a very tough five-game match. On the other side of the bracket, Oklahoma upset Nebraska to reach the regional final. But the Sooners seemed content with beating Nebraska and didn't pose much of a threat for us the next night. We won 3-0, Laura Bush serving a string of aces in the third game. The crowd kept getting louder and louder, and by the end of the match, the Oklahoma passers weren't even coming close to the ball.

So here we were in the Final Four again, and the toughest hurdle along the way had been Notre Dame. In stark contrast to the previous year's blood, sweat, and tears, particularly that monumental Western Michigan match, we'd just waltzed home. If there was ever a year when we got the breaks and the bounces in the playoffs, it was '88.

The Final Four was in Minneapolis, and we drew Hawaii again. We had played them tough the year before and were confident we could beat them. It was the biggest crowd ever to see a Final Four match, and it was our time. Or maybe not.

One play at the start of the Hawaii match set the tone for the entire night. Petra Laverman was playing the left side for us and we were serving. Hawaii overpassed right to Petra. Inexplicably, instead of hitting the ball, Petra grabbed it in a two-handed dunk and threw it right into the net. Instead of an easy point, the first one of the match, it was a sideout, and Hawaii went on to pound us 15-1.

Once we put that first-game debacle behind us, it became a dead-even match. We lost the second game 15-12, then came back and won the third 15-13. Mary Eggers and Nancy Brookhart, both in their prime, playing in the spotlight, performed extremely well. It was one of the most focused matches I've ever seen Brookhart play, and Eggers, in her last chance, was consumed with wanting to win a championship.

Barb Winsett had a very difficult match, and Bridget Boyle was inconsistent, but our Achilles' heel, as it had been for the entire season, was the other left-side position. Petra had started the season with a bang, recording 26 kills against UCLA in her first U.S. collegiate match. Now three months later, I had to take her out of the match. I tried Dillman, I spent the entire night fishing around trying to find someone to play well. Despite that, we came within an eyelash of rallying in that match.

We did a good job of neutralizing Hawaii's top performer, Teee Williams, but we got beaten by Carolyn Taetofa, who had something like 21 kills. She hadn't really put up the numbers over the year, so our game plan had been to take care of Williams and hope we could contain the others. Well, we didn't contain Taetofa. We were tied late in the fourth game and could have won it, but we lost 15-13, and that was that. Had we won the fourth game, I am convinced we would have won the match.

The season was over, the season when we were supposed to win our national championship. And we could have won it. UCLA was beatable, Texas was beatable, so was Hawaii. But obviously, so were we. After the match, Mary Eggers was absolutely devastated, but it was the closest we'd come — and still the closest we've come — to grabbing the brass ring. To this day, I wonder what would have happened had Barb Winsett been healthy. It was like trying to win a basketball championship with a point guard playing on one leg.

Regrets aside, following the '88 season, I felt pretty good about our program. We had become the dominant team in the Mideast Region. We had been to two consecutive NCAA Final Fours. We were one of the top three or four programs in the nation, taking everything into account — level of play, crowds, media attention. We were right there with Hawaii, Pacific, Nebraska.

Maybe I developed a touch of benign neglect toward the little things that had gotten us where we were. It wasn't intentional, but I began to make some assumptions, rather than aggressively pursuing things to see that they were done right. I should have paid closer attention when we had two subpar recruiting classes in a row, for example. And I certainly should have done a better job of dealing with the transition from Don Hardin to Jay Potter, both quality assistants, but ones with different recruiting and coaching styles.

The 1989, '90 and '91 seasons are difficult to talk about because I was starting to get burned out. I was increasing the division of labor among my staff because I was getting really tired. The atmosphere around the program began to change — I wasn't making every decision, calling every shot. I was becoming more of a distant, hands-off coach. I even began to step back in practice, sort of a Bear Bryant, bullhorn-from-the-tower style. I wanted to give my staff input and keep everyone happy. Chuck Erbe had joined the staff, and I wanted Jay and Chuck and Beth Launiere, our graduate assistant coach, to feel a part of what was going on. So, sometimes willingly, sometimes grudgingly, I took a step back from the center of things. In retrospect, I think it was a mistake.

Having Chuck Erbe join our staff was an interesting twist. Throughout his career, Chuck marched to his own drumbeat and did things his own way. He never invited a lot of outside feedback or direction. Why should he? He had won four national titles at Southern Cal doing things his way. I think Chuck became a victim of changing times at USC. The kids were changing, attitudes were changing, the whole historical perspective of what he had accomplished was beginning to change. As volleyball came more and more under the microscope of the NCAA and the governing bodies, what Chuck accomplished was going to be less and less possible.

His style had been to burrow into the gym and hibernate there and train athletes for hours and hours every day. That approach was extremely successful, but after a while the transformation of the collegiate environment made it unworkable. The young players just couldn't live with that anymore. Chuck had juggled all the demands of his position very well for a long time, but he finally got to the point where he couldn't adapt quickly enough.

When he hit the wall, I think Chuck looked around and found that he had isolated himself from the rest of the collegiate coaching community. Many of us had been working hard to establish the American Volleyball Coaches Association and serving on committees and networking with each other, but Chuck had basically declared that he was going to go it alone. That worked fine until he needed help, and then not too many people knew him.

Several of us had remained close to Chuck over the years, though, and I was one of them. I like Chuck, and I might not have gotten the Illinois job if not for him. He also gave me a shot at

Orbiting in Ohio   139

coaching at the international level, taking me to Romania in 1981. Chuck does things differently than I do, but that's not a problem. I owe Chuck a lot, and when he was cut loose by USC in early 1989, I asked him to join us until he landed another head coaching job. We'd just gotten approval for a second assistant's position, and Chuck signed on.

It was more of a personal decision for Chuck than a professional one. Obviously, he didn't have anything to prove. But he had put his personal growth on hold for years while he was making this superman effort to become the volleyball czar of the U.S. He told me, "Everything has gone wrong here. I want to get out of California. I want to get someplace like the Midwest, where the pace of life is a little slower and there are more values. I want to go back to school." So we worked it out and Chuck came to Illinois to coach and to take over our recruiting efforts.

Naturally, when you can get a guy like Chuck Erbe, it's a great addition to your staff, but tossing him into the mix led to some complications, too. Chuck had always been used to running things, and I was looking for a way to give everyone a chance. More and more, my role became keeping both Chuck and Jay happy in the gym. Ultimately, I spent way too much time on that and not nearly enough time keeping the team on track. These were two talented guys, each with his own style, his own way of doing things, and they needed a mediator. They never confronted each other in a hostile way or with any animosity, but it was clear they frustrated each other.

Trying to work out these staff problems put a strain on the 1989 team, and so did my taking a step back to reduce the stress and fatigue in my life. Nevertheless, coming into the season, we figured to have an excellent team, led by Nancy Brookhart, Bridget Boyle and Laura Bush. We had Barb Winsett back as a junior setter, with Petra Laverman hitting on the left side. But when practice started in the fall, Bush and Brookhart, our two All-America middle blockers, came back with serious knee problems. Nancy was recovering from surgery to repair cartilage damage, and Laura had developed very serious patellar tendinitis. Neither of those injuries got any better, so we practiced that entire season without our two starting middle blockers. A lot of coaches say things like that, but I am not exaggerating. Those two practiced maybe two or three times all season, and they didn't go very hard.

Nancy did all she could on the sidelines, but you can't ride the exercise bike forever, and you can't get game-ready by doing calisthenics. Even her conditioning work suffered because of the injury. We took her to the early tournaments just to see what she could do, figure out what we could expect from her. Later on, when we had Friday and Saturday matches, it was always a guessing game. Sometimes Nancy would be up to playing both nights, but other times she could only play one match in a weekend. So every week we'd look at our upcoming schedule and puzzle over it: "When do we play Nancy, and how long?"

Laura wasn't much better. She hardly ever practiced, and in matches, her knee would get inflamed after just a few minutes. We'd take her out for a back-row substitute and get ice on her knee immediately while she was waiting to go back in. Brookhart was the same way. It was extremely frustrating for Nancy and Laura and for the staff. No one held it against them — these kids were hurt. If anything, I really admired them for gutting it out that season. But not having them in practice, not being able to count on them all the time in matches — that was devastating to our hopes for the Big Ten and NCAA championships.

Even with our setter and two top middle blockers nursing serious knee injuries, the Big Ten coaches picked us to win the conference title. Instead we went 13-5 in the Big Ten, 27-8 overall, falling one step short of the Final Four.

We got off to a great start, losing only to UCLA, 3-2, in the championship of the SportMart Classic in Chicago. On September 23, we made history again when Minnesota came to Kenney Gym for a nationally televised match on ESPN. We hosted Minnesota with a 33-match home winning streak on the line. Minnesota played well, we played well, and we had a 2-1 lead when Minnesota rallied to win the fourth game 15-12.

With the three bad knees, long matches were trouble for us all season. Jay and I discussed it all the time: "If we get into a long match, we're in big trouble, because our middles can't play hard at the end." I had to take Nancy out because her knees were hurting so bad she could barely jump — in fact, she could barely move. Of course, nobody knew that — you don't announce it because you don't want to appear to be making excuses. But we lost the match primarily because our two top performers were unable to perform very well.

Orbiting in Ohio

Minnesota became the team that broke our home winning streak, and they went berserk, like they had won the national title. I don't blame them; we'd have had the same reaction had we been in their place. That was the magnitude of the loss for us. I remember looking at our team after the match, particularly Bush and Brookhart. They were just devastated by the loss, of course, but they were also in terrible pain. They could barely move afterward, but nobody outside the team knew how bad it was. They were warriors — take a break, ice it down, then hobble back on court.

The same thing hurt us the next week at Ohio State — but we clearly weren't meant to win that match under any circumstances. The night before, we had put Bridget Boyle in the middle and moved Lisa Dillman to the left side in beating Indiana 3-0 in Bloomington. Both of them played a great match. We rested Brookhart and Bush and got by with a makeshift lineup. As the bus left the hotel the next night in Columbus, we were talking about how to use Dillman against Ohio State. Suddenly Jan Ochsenwald, our trainer, came up, a worried look on her face. Jan didn't know what was wrong, but Lisa had come down with a fever and the shakes.

Meanwhile, OSU's football game had just ended, and we were trying to get to St. John Arena against Ohio Stadium traffic. We kept circling the campus, turning into drives to get to the gym, only to have policemen wave us out. We tried to explain our situation — not only do we have a match scheduled, we also have a sick player who's not getting any better being bounced around on the bus. Nobody wanted to hear about it. "But we're playing at St. John." "I don't care, get the hell out of here."

We had been circling for close to an hour when we finally stopped the bus, got out and confronted a patrolman. I said, "Look, we've got a contract to play at St. John Arena. I don't care who you have to call, the athletic director, officials of the arena, whoever, but please, call somebody and help us out." He looked right at me and said, "If you don't get this goddamned bus out of here, you're going to be under arrest."

I wouldn't give up. "I understand what your job is," I said, "but we play in 45 minutes." I gave him the whole story, and he told me to wait there. Great, I thought, finally somebody's going to help us. Instead, he came back with his superior officer, who started writing down the number of the bus. He pointed his finger at me and said, "You guys are in big trouble." I jumped back on the bus and told the driver to get moving. It was now 63 minutes on the bus for what should have been a 10-minute ride, and we were still just orbiting campus.

I swear I was almost ready to turn back at this point, just head for Champaign, but when you're a coach, there's a protocol that says you've got to do everything humanly possible to make the match. How far do you push it? When do you just say, "I can't do any more"? I wasn't sure, but I knew I didn't want to create a political problem for Karol. I didn't want to put her in the position of having to explain to their AD why our team didn't ever show up for the match. Those things tend to mushroom way out of proportion, accusations hurled back and forth. So we were going to do everything we could within the law to get to St. John. Scratch that—we were going to do everything we could, period.

I told the driver to slow down on High Street as we approached Lane Street to make the turn to the arena. There were barricades across the street, so I jumped out and started tossing them off to the side. By this time, I'd snapped. Match time was 7:30, and it was already past 7. I've got Dillman in the back of the bus throwing up, my two middle blockers are icing their knees, we're supposed to be playing this critical Big Ten match and they won't let us get to the gym. I was throwing the last barricade aside and waving the bus driver through, players leaning out the windows cheering me on, when a policeman came running up the street toward me. The driver wheeled around the corner down Lane Street — the wrong way. He popped the door open, I hopped on and he stepped on the gas. I had one leg on the bus, one leg out the door, it was the Charge of the Light Brigade. The bus driver was psyched, the team was screaming — if we had been on horseback, there'd have been bugles sounding the charge. All the policeman could do was stand and watch as we pulled away.

Once we got past that barrier, it was clear sailing. When we finally pulled up to St. John Arena, 20 minutes from match time, everybody was completely frazzled. We had broken the law, literally broken through the lines to get to this match, and the last thing we had our minds on now was volleyball. We walked into the arena and Jim Stone, the OSU coach, came up and said, "Hey, what happened?" "Don't ask. Let's just get it going—we'll be out as soon as we can."

Orbiting in Ohio

They gave us a few extra minutes to get ready, and when the match started, Jan stayed in the locker room with Lisa, who was lying on a bench with cold compresses on her head. Lisa was ultimately diagnosed as having viral encephalitis, a serious illness. So we came out worried about her, of course, but beyond that, we were missing three players *and* our trainer. We were on our own. We put a patchwork lineup together and we played like we felt, frazzled, but we nearly pulled it off. We lost 3-2, and Ohio State went berserk. It was like that all season long — we kept watching these other teams celebrating. We had played well, but the injuries were killing us.

The Ohio State loss really sent me reeling. We had won 53 out of 54 matches in the Big Ten over a three-year period, and losing was something we'd forgotten how to deal with. Now we were vulnerable, we were wounded, and two teams had picked us off. One week into the 1989 Big Ten race and we had already lost two matches. "This is what happens," I realized, "when you *don't* have the luck on your side, when you *don't* get the breaks. I've got to prepare myself for this."

Something else I hadn't realized was the depth of frustration in the conference over our domination the previous three seasons. I hadn't really taken much time to look over my shoulder to check on the welfare of the teams we were beating. When Ohio State beat us later at Kenney Gym, I overheard one of their players telling reporters how much the victory meant. "Yeah, it's great," she said. "We're just so sick of 'Illinois, Illinois, Illinois.'" I didn't think it was a very classy thing to say to the press, but at the same time I began to understand what she meant. We'd been dominating so long and the other teams had been working so hard, it was a rush for them finally to get over the hump.

We got a third shot at the Buckeyes. We finished the regular season 25-7, so we made the NCAA tournament despite all our troubles. Then we beat Penn State 3-1 in the opening round and got Ohio State in the Mideast semifinals in Lincoln. OSU had dethroned us as Big Ten champion, but this time we played one of the best matches that we've ever put together at Illinois, one of our guttiest performances. We won 3-1, taking the fourth game 17-15. After a year of bad draws, bad injuries, just bad business in general, we got a few breaks, and winning that match made the entire season worthwhile.

We didn't have anything left for our next match, against Nebraska. We led the first game 14-12 when Bush knocked an overpass out of bounds that would have won it. Once we lost the first game, the team just melted, losing 3-0. That was a good Nebraska team, though; even healthy, we'd have been stretched pretty far to beat them. As it was, Nancy was finished, having given her all against Ohio State, and we weren't the same team without her. I was really proud of that group, though. Finally we'd had a season where all the breaks went against us, but we never gave up. We were sure we could bounce back, but in fact, worse times were ahead.

ROCK BOTTOM

Fourteen years. I'd been coaching college volleyball for 14 years now, and, from the time at Pitt when I'd realized I wanted to make it my career, I had never questioned that this was where I belonged. I'd done pretty darned well, made a name for my teams, made a name for myself. The '89 season had been disappointing, but it was just a glitch — the injuries were something that you could never plan for, they were just going to get you sometimes; the personality problems were something to learn from and do better in the future. It was just an off season, nobody's fault — and an "off" season where we still went 27-8 and made it to the regional final.

The next two seasons were something else again. I did a lot of soul-searching during 1990 and '91 about whether I wanted to remain in coaching. I questioned our recruiting approach, I questioned my own abilities, my confidence was rattled. I came very close to resigning, not out of any resentment or anger toward anyone, but just from what was inside me. The lifestyle of a coach is so stressful. Did I want to continue to endure the pressure? And am I still good enough, do I still have it? We went 21-12 and 19-10 those seasons, so it was hard to call them total disasters, but to me that's just what they were. And it wasn't just losing that hurt, it was the *way* we lost.

It seemed like the worst thing we could do in 1990 was win the first two games in a match. Four times that season, we got up 2-0 only to let the match get away. It started in the Illini Classic. We were 3-0 and playing Stanford for the Classic title. We won the first two games 15-10 and 15-8, and we were rolling 7-0 in the third when our All-America middle blocker Laura Bush went down with a shoulder separation. Bush was our aircraft carrier at that point, she was carrying us on the court. Stanford outscored us 30-4 to even the match, then won the fifth game 15-10.

I think that one match turned around the Stanford program. The year before, the Cardinals had gone through the same sort of season we were about to go through. They couldn't put one foot in front of the other without making a mistake. They had all these All- Americans — Bev Oden, Kristin Klein, Amy Cooper — and they were something like 18-16. Three years later, that same Stanford team won the NCAA title. If Bush hadn't gotten hurt, if we'd been able to keep the thumb down on them in that match, what would have happened? Stanford would have caught fire at some point, but maybe not as fast. And I know we'd have been better off.

It was shaping up as a difficult season, too, because of politics. We were trying to blend five freshmen with a senior class, and we were meeting some resistance. I started working freshman Merrill Mullis into the setter position as Barb Winsett's knee continued to deteriorate. Suddenly the community adopted Barb, made a martyr of her. I took some flak from the fans over that. "You don't treat seniors that way," seemed to be the attitude. Well, I've always felt you play whoever's doing the job. What's going to win the match has to be what guides you, and given the condition of Barb's knee, we had to get Merrill in there. But you don't say to the press, "This player's ability had declined so she won't be in there as much." There have been other players the community has fallen in love with and thought should be getting more playing time. And sometimes they don't measure up in terms of ability, contributions to team chemistry, and so on. But again, you can't say that.

Our freshman class — Kristin Henriksen, Kellie Hebeisen, Tina Rogers, Merrill Mullis and Amy Jones — had been named the nation's top recruiting class by *Volleyball Monthly,* but they all had a lot to learn. Each of them was very talented, but every one had serious weaknesses in her game. One might be weak on defense, the next might need to work on blocking, maybe this one needed to learn how to pass. They all needed a lot of work, but when people read "top recruiting class in the country," it's a double-edged sword: expectations rise to unrealistic levels.

And even aside from the weaknesses people weren't aware of, these were freshmen. We'd had a freshman come along once who could elevate the program immediately, who couldn't

Rock Bottom

just play, but who could handle the mental demands and pull everything together. Unfortunately, nobody in this group was Mary Eggers. We had good kids but they needed a lot of work, and they needed leadership from the senior class. They weren't getting it.

So our project of blending the freshmen and seniors into a good team was foundering, and because of those subpar recruiting years in '88 and '89, there wasn't much in between. The junior class wasn't contributing anything, between defections and injuries. The sophomore class consisted of two players, Anne Conway and Lorna Henderson. We didn't have the guns anymore, and the other Big Ten teams knew it. We were giving off the scent of defeat, and the other teams were going into a feeding frenzy. All of a sudden Wisconsin emerged as the Big Ten's powerhouse, and Ohio State and Minnesota moved past us, too.

The players we had relied on in the glory years were gone, and the inability of the remaining players to lead and to set the tone was exposed for the first time. They were fun kids to be around — I loved Lisa Dillman's sense of humor, Laura Bush's dry wit — but in terms of team dynamics, things just never came together. We won some key matches, and the crowd went crazy when we beat Ohio State, but it seemed like we didn't really go out and cause it to happen, it was just our turn to get a few breaks.

Two weeks after letting Stanford off the ropes in the Illini Classic, we blew 2-0 leads against Nebraska and Pacific in the Illini Invitational. That became an enduring and maddening theme of the season. We went into a tailspin. A month later, we had a 2-0 lead at Wisconsin, trying to slow the Badgers' march to the Big Ten title. We lost.

Every coach has a season to forget, I guess, and this was mine. I kept pushing buttons and pulling strings and nothing would work. It all came down to not having the senior leadership. We didn't have anybody on the team who could say, like Eggers used to, or Disa Johnson, or Fracaro or Brookhart, "When it matters, we'll win the match." So when the breaks didn't go their way and their confidence was jarred, they didn't have anybody to give them that emotional slap in the face that says, "Hey, we're better than this — let's go get after it." That's what 1990 was all about.

We made the NCAA tournament again, but about all we accomplished there was to get into the record book as a footnote. Our first-round assignment was at Wisconsin, where Steve Lowe had won a Big Ten championship and made Badger volleyball an overnight sensation. Steve told me they were expecting "over 5,000" for the match. It was over 5,000, all right: an NCAA-record 10,935 came to watch us play in the UW Fieldhouse.

Our team reached the playoffs beaten up, both physically and mentally, and led by a frustrated coach. I was unaccustomed to not having the right things happen when I pushed the buttons I knew I was supposed to push. We shanked the first serve of the game into the crowd, and we were never in the match. My team was playing in front of the largest crowd in NCAA history, and we were backing away from the challenge. A great performance, even if we'd lost, could have atoned for so much. The seniors, Winsett, Bush and Dillman, had come to me before the match to say, "Give us the ball, we'll take it home," but they just couldn't do it. The glove had been thrown down, and we didn't respond to it.

I tried everything—Tina Rogers was on the right side, I'd gone back to Winsett setting, nothing worked. Nothing could have punctuated that season more aptly than seeing our great freshman middle blocker, Kristin Henriksen, carried off the floor with a freak shoulder separation. That was it.

What had gone wrong? Well, I see two possibilities: one, I didn't know enough to put that group on the right track, and I'll readily take that blame; or two, I did my job, gave the team what it needed to win, but the group didn't take the hook. I honestly don't know which one it was, or whether it was a combination of the two.

All I knew at the time was that something had to change. I met with Jay Potter, Disa Johnson, who was now our second assistant, and Kathy Cunningham, our graduate assistant, and I wanted to hear everything they thought was wrong with the program—what had been going on, what needed to be corrected if we were going to win again. I took down all of their suggestions, added my own and came up with a list of 48 items that had to be changed for our program to get back on track. And during the next week — when it had become our custom to be at the regional championship — I held a team meeting, a three-hour meeting, to tell the returning players what we were going to do.

Not many of the items were performance-related; most had to do with activities off the court. For example, I had gotten the feeling that our boosters weren't feeling good about the program anymore. Our players weren't going out of their way to

Rock Bottom

say thank you. That was one of the 48 points: just talk to the boosters and fans, and when someone does something nice for you, say "thank you." That's how basic some of this stuff was, just common courtesy or common sense. Some of the other points had to do with academics, where some of the players weren't taking care of business.

What it came down to was that the players were taking advantage of the program and its perks, the great uniform contract, all the little things that were done for UI volleyball, and they weren't giving anything in return. And as coach I knew I shared responsibility for what had gone wrong. But at that meeting, I made it clear that it was time to put things back together. These 48 things needed to be done to get us back on track. Something had gotten broken somewhere along the line, and now we were going to fix it.

We started from scratch, relearning principles we'd taken for granted for so long we'd begun to ignore them. And I learned never to take those things for granted again. Now we go over these points every year, no matter how settled and mature I think the team may be. These are the things we have to do to win and be a quality program. Everyone who goes through the program has to know what it means to be an Illini volleyball player.

Not long after that meeting, I unveiled a 22-month plan to get us back to the Final Four. Where the 48 points dealt mostly with things the players had to do on a personal and community level, this dealt with what we had to do as a coaching staff to bring about success on the floor. A lot of it involved getting tougher with the athletes on and off the court, improving their work habits and discipline. The plan was broken down into phases and levels of success, all pointing to winning the 1992 Big Ten title and going back to the Final Four. We almost got there, but we still had plenty of frustration ahead of us.

I started taking the reins of practice more, not because I didn't think Jay and Disa could handle it, but because, if I was going to go down, if my teams weren't going to be any good any more, there was going to be nobody to blame but me. It was very important to reestablish a firm grip on every aspect of the program. My back was against the wall, and I wanted to come out swinging.

I worked hard on recruiting in the off-season, and we signed another excellent class of athletes: Sue Nucci, Kathleen Shannon, Amy Brickley and Julie Edwards. Once again, it was selected as the nation's top recruiting class by *Volleyball Monthly*. And once again, it was a class loaded with talent, but also hampered by severe deficiencies. Defense, blocking, passing, hitting — everybody had at least one Achilles' heel, and some had a matching set.

But that was OK. With no seniors and only two juniors, it was time for a new team and a new program. I already knew I had to start teaching from scratch. Everything I'd built before, I had to build again. The '91 season was a struggle, but it was a different kind of struggle. I knew we wouldn't be dominating, and while I was unhappy with the lack of discipline and competitiveness of the team, I knew that it was because these young players hadn't been shown the way how to be tough at the college level. That was something we planned to fix with that 22-month plan.

It's hard for people to fathom now, but as freshmen in 1990, Merrill Mullis, Tina Rogers, and Kellie Hebeisen would literally refuse to go the floor to play defense. The three of them scoffed at that, considered it inappropriate behavior. They had never been made to work like that as junior players. So that's where we started. I remember sending Disa over to work with them to teach them how to go the floor and getting these dagger glares from that side of the floor. This was cruel and unusual punishment, as far as they were concerned. It was like, "Who do you think you are making me do this? Don't you know who I am? Haven't you read my press clippings?"

The '91 season was frustrating because we lost some matches that I knew we should be winning, but I didn't question our direction. I knew that our 22-month plan was in place and that we'd have to take some lumps along the way as we continued to teach and learn. What I didn't realize was how far we were from consolidating as a group, establishing a team chemistry. I also didn't realize how good Ohio State and Penn State would be. In retrospect, though, I think the worst thing about '91 was that I was still smarting from '90.

We had begun to pull together late in the season and had won a key match at Northwestern heading into the regular-season finale at Wisconsin. A win over the Badgers would give us a first-round NCAA match at home. We lost the first two games, then rallied to send the match to a fifth game. The NCAA had gone to fifth-game rally scoring, where a point is scored on every serve, even on what would ordinarily just be a sideout. We were in a position to win in the rally scoring, but Kathleen Shannon served out of bounds, and then Sue Nucci went up for her favorite shot and hit it into Row 8. It was a tough loss, but we were relying on freshmen at crunch time, people who needed to learn how to handle pressure.

After that loss, we not only didn't host a first-round NCAA match, we were given an unbelievably bad seed, having to play at Nebraska. We had beaten Wisconsin 3-0 at home early in the year, then lost a tough match there late, but they got seeded higher. They also hadn't played as tough a schedule overall as we had, but they got to host Bowling Green while we packed our bags for Lincoln — a pretty severe penalty for losing 18-16 in the fifth game.

We went to Nebraska, and we didn't even compete. When I evaluate a team, I don't ask whether it's good enough to make the NCAA tournament but rather how competitive that team can be in the tournament. In 1990 and '91, we were not a quality tournament team. Those were our two worst performances in the NCAA tournament, our only first-round losses, and both in three games.

My last team at New Mexico was like those '90 and '91 Illinois teams, a group that just could not or would not compete in a tough situation. These teams were extremely difficult to push out of their comfort zone. It was like they were on a bungee cord. I could only stretch them so far out of the comfort zone before they'd snap back. I was about ready to snap, too.

I came very close to resigning after that season, interviewing with more than a handful of people in other professions. I had several invitations to enter business. I talked to Sherry about my future and what it would be like without coaching. I just didn't want to put myself through the level of stress I had allowed this job to put me through in 1990 and '91. But I elected to stay with it — for better or for worse, I was a coach.

We knew in 1991 that by December of 1992, we would have a strong junior class and a strong sophomore class. We had taken a trip to Puerto Rico in the spring of '91, and now the master plan called for a summer trip to Europe in '92. Planning that trip in the spring was just what I needed, and just what the team needed. It created a lot of positive energy and got everybody's focus off of the negative experiences of the previous two seasons. It gave us something to look forward to.

The European trip was a complete success for our program, in every respect, starting with public relations. Just as the program needed renewal, so did our fan support. So we got them involved in the European trip from the first. We had a "bowl-a-thon," a one-day promotion and fund-raiser, at GT's Western Bowl, owned by our good friend Bill Green. The idea was to collect pledges for the trip, per pin, for each participant. The three-game series would be added up, and the players, coaches and celebrities would collect the pledge money. Several local celebrities pitched in, radio and television personalities, even Lou Henson helped out.

It was even more successful as a fund-raiser than we'd expected, but it also got everyone, players and community alike, thinking about the European tour. The bowl-a-thon was a great mental preparation tool for our players. We prepared them on the court, too, putting them through 10 physically demanding days of practice right before we left. We really wanted the team to toughen up. We put a lot of energy into the European trip, and our goal was to make the matches the easy part and the day-in, day-out training the difficult part.

But we weren't concerned only with what they did on the floor. We hadn't forgotten the 48 points. We wanted to see the team come together *as* a team, we wanted to see the players conduct themselves admirably as Americans and as representatives of the University of Illinois, and we weren't disappointed. They began to display some unselfish traits we hadn't seen before, a willingness to forego some comforts for the good of the team.

One of the ways players have changed since I started coaching is that the younger generation seems to take so much more for granted. I know I sound like a middle-aged parent, but it's true. I remember the early days of college volleyball, when the players had to buy their own shoes, and maybe we were given one set of hand-me-down basketball warm-ups, and one or two game uniforms for the season. And those kids just thought how wonderful it was to practice and play the game, it didn't matter if there was shampoo in the hotels or you couldn't get pickles on your hamburger. Now I see kids spending so much more time asking, "What's in it for me?" and "Why isn't this the way I want it to be?" and "What kind of place is this Aarhus, Denmark, if it doesn't even have a McDonald's?" It's ethnocentrism, of course.

Rock Bottom 153

I think given the environment they're raised in, these are good kids, but today's environment is so different from the one the earlier kids came from.

Naturally it follows that today's kids are much less equipped on their own to decide how they're going to pursue their athletic goals with class and integrity and determination. They're myopic about what's required to accomplish their goals. It's always, "This makes me uncomfortable, why do I have to do this?" or "Why isn't someone doing this for me, why do I have to do it myself?" So, taking off on a trip to Europe, I was concerned with seeing what was going to happen when these modern-day kids arrived somewhere where no one spoke English and they wanted to find a bathroom. How would they deal with that situation? I found out that this team was made up of very quick learners who knew how to adapt.

Living out of a suitcase, spending half your time on a bus, thrown together with a bunch of people in tight conditions and strange surroundings for three weeks — that would put a strain on any relationship. As a team, they also had to compete, never mind that you just got off the bus and just want to lie down. This team did a superb job of handling those hardships, of making the tough times draw them together as a team rather than drive them apart.

And that was part of our plan, too. The idea was to give our players some perspective, to put them in an environment that afterward would make them think that the travel and the routines of college volleyball were a breeze. We also wanted them to expand their horizons by playing against different styles and higher levels of competition. If you've played a top Belgian club team in Brussels, then it's no big deal when you have to go to Ann Arbor and play Michigan during the season.

When we got to Europe, my questions about what kind of team we were going to have were answered immediately. The players were much more confident, accountable to one another, working together in a way we hadn't seen the previous fall. In the first match of the tour, we played the Dutch Junior National team. It was a difficult situation — we were jet-lagged and tired, playing in an empty gym, using a different ball in completely strange surroundings against a good Dutch team. We fell behind 2-1 and it would have been easy to throw in the towel, say, "So long, we're out of here." But the team battled back and won the match. This was something we hadn't seen from this group before, a really important building block for us.

None of our success was an accident. It never is. We knew who we wanted to play on our three-week trip — we'd started making contacts a year earlier to get the right type of competition. But it was gratifying, maybe even a little surprising, to see things working exactly as we'd hoped. We lost a close match the next night to the same Dutch team, but that was because I did a lot of substituting. Then we ran off eight victories in a row, while coping with all kinds of different circumstances, languages and situations.

Meanwhile, back home people were keeping up with our progress, and the public relations boost we got from the "bowl-a-thon" was snowballing. When you're on a European tour, you're often just looking around asking what's next. You are so involved in the experience, the practices and competition, you forget that people back in Champaign-Urbana are picking up a newspaper at the grocery store to see whether our team won or lost 4,000 miles away.

I remember talking to Stevie Jay on WDWS radio one morning from the Eurovolley Center in Belgium. When Stevie would ask a question, I really had to step back and think about what people in Champaign-Urbana wanted to hear about. They didn't want to hear about how I'd spent the last 30 minutes trying to figure out what kind of coin goes into this machine so that we can wash some uniforms. Or that we're not sure if the guy downstairs, the one trying to tell us how to get to the restaurant, is speaking German or French or what. The things you're experiencing on the trip don't prepare you for the types of questions you hear from the breakfast show back home. The people at home want to know who we played, whether we won or lost, how practice is coming along, who's playing well. Who did we play? I don't know, I don't even know how to pronounce the name, much less remember who it is.

In 21 days, we played 10 matches in Holland, Belgium, Denmark and Germany. We had tough competition, even tougher practices, and we had time for some sightseeing and other outings. I knew from other international tours how important that was. I had been on trips where we had worked on volleyball 10 hours every day. You just can't do that physically, not with a college team. I wanted to include some cultural experiences, some museums and historical landmarks, and I also wanted to have some days that were just for fun, when they could just forget volleyball.

Still, this was as hard as I've worked a college team for a sustained time. With international teams, it's a different type of training. Those players are used to working much harder, and they get right into it. This team still has to be coaxed up to the level of play we expected from them. The fun days not only softened the demands of practices and games, they threw the players together in a social situation, where they could get to know each other as friends and classmates instead of parts of this goal-oriented machine. And by getting to know each other *off* the court, they would be that much closer when they got back *on* the court. Hanging out just as a gang of American college students made them that much more a team.

That team feeling would stay with the team all year long, and so would the confidence that was just starting to grow. We came back to start the '92 season with a whole new outlook. And on top of that, we had a wild card, Dutch Olympian Kirsten Gleis, to add to the deck.

CHAPTER 14

BACK WHERE WE BELONG

If a coach has even one moment in his or her career like I experienced when I got off the plane returning from Europe — the Networkers, the fans, the alumni, the band, the whole community out to welcome us home — it's something you can carry around and treasure. While I've been at Illinois, I have had hundreds of moments like that, and I treasure them all.

As I often tell the Networkers, our support group, we never take that support for granted, and we never will. I still sit on the bench at matches and wonder who all of these people are. How far did they drive to see us play? An hour, 10 minutes? What possessed this person to get the family together, get in the car and come see my team play? It's always amazing to me.

On the short flight from Chicago to Champaign, the last leg of our trip, we all just wanted to lie down and sleep for a week. Anybody who's ever flown back from overseas knows how exhausting it is. But once we learned that people were waiting for us at the airport, a light switch seemed to go on for our players. We'd gone 9-1 on the trip, and knowing that there was a reception planned for us made us think, "Maybe we've really accomplished something; maybe we can be pretty good."

The minute the team walked through the doors into the airport lounge, I could see everyone's fatigue melt away. Kristin Henriksen's face lit up, Amy Brickley broke into a grin, everybody was just regenerated. Seeing the fans, the alums, Dan Perino and his Medicare 7, 8 or 9 band — you just wanted to thank the whole community. Lou Henson had just returned from a trip, and he stuck around to meet the team. Lou is one of the really nice guys of all time. He has been so generous to me and to our program, showing genuine attention and appreciation for our accomplishments. And now he was part of this great welcoming committee, making us feel like we were champions before the season had even begun.

Now it was time to justify that support. I had seen a light go on in Europe. We had pinned down our two passers in Julie Edwards and Lorna Henderson. Our setting had begun to improve to the point where we could count on some offensive efficiency again. Remember, Illinois was an offensive giant through the 1980s, but in '90 and '91, we plummeted offensively, hitting from .218 to .225 as a team. A lot of the drop-off was due to our hitters, but our setting was also very inconsistent, and so was our passing. Overnight in Europe, our passing game improved, our setting became efficient, and we hit at a .295 clip. For team offense, anything over .275 is really good. Anything over .300 as a team is spectacular. We ended up 1992 hitting .328, a school record. We saw those things begin to happen in Europe, the passing, the setting, the hitting.

The trip also answered our two biggest questions. Could Tina Rogers become a big-time player in a new position? And could Kristin Henriksen play at all after off-season shoulder and knee surgery?

As a freshman, Tina had done all right as a right-side hitter. We just wanted to put a big body on that side of the net, and at 6-foot-3 she fit the bill. As a sophomore, Tina endured a sophomore slump. She played tentatively, missed several matches with injuries and never really came around. There were several matches we either didn't start her or took her out because she wasn't effective. So, heading to Europe, we were looking at a player with great promise who had gone backward in her development. At the same time, we needed another left-side hitter, so we thought we'd experiment with Tina. Could she hit the ball over there?

Kristin had had shoulder surgery and sat out the entire spring. Then she had knee surgery and further shoulder problems. She practiced very little during the July workouts before we left for Europe. For a question mark, Kristin had quite a season. She very nearly led the nation in hitting efficiency and was a standout all year long.

Back Where We Belong 159

Tina Rogers became an All-Big Ten pick and a second-team All-American, and Kristin Henriksen just missed being an All-American. Can you imagine that both players were both gigantic "IFs" heading into the European tour? Tina came through big on the European trip and began to gain confidence hitting the ball from the left side, and Kristin started using her shoulder with no pain and getting stronger and stronger.

That brings me to two things I want to emphasize about Kirsten Gleis' contributions to our 1992 season. First, this was already a confident team that could have won the Big Ten. Not only had we answered the question mark about Kristin Henrikson's health and found that Julie Edwards was beginning to live up to her full potential, but everybody was a year older, and I could see this group of sophomores and juniors maturing. They were starting to feel a little more at home with the burden of carrying the Illinois program. They were starting to care more about what they were doing on and off the floor. There's no question Kirsten accelerated what was already taking place and elevated the team another notch or two. But Illinois was already going to be a much different team from the previous two years. That point gets lost in the shuffle when people talk about Kirsten's presence and what she did for the program.

Nobody believes the second point, but I swear this is genuine. A lot of people think it was a smoke screen when I said that Kirsten Gleis was an average international player and I didn't know how good she was going to be. I had only seen her play at the international level, and, while I had coached some international teams, it's difficult to project from international play how good a player will be at the collegiate level.

I said things like, "There is a possibility that Kirsten could start for us." I honestly didn't know whether she could beat out Julie Edwards, because I'd never seen her pass for Holland. On the Dutch team, two other players did the passing. We found out she's a great passer, and we made her a primary passer, but when we got her, I'd never seen her pass. That is the difference in the level of play between international volleyball and the women's college game — somebody who's just one of the team there can come here and be a star.

Part of that is just the high level of talent in Europe, but in Kirsten's case, at least, I think it was also the liberating effect of being *allowed* to be a star. Here was a player on the Dutch National team who hardly ever got a set or swung at the ball in a match. She had been the last offensive option for the Dutch in the Olympics. When she came to Illinois and was given a leading role in our offense, it was like she'd been let out of her cage. She got to do everything with us, and that excited her, and both those factors helped her to become, very quickly, the great player she'd always had the potential to be.

But when she showed up, I didn't know what role she would play. I thought she would be our right-side hitter, but I wasn't sure. We tried several different things to see how she would fit in. Our offense is designed around the talents of our personnel, and until we saw Kirsten in action, we didn't know what position she would play or what style we would use. It became clear after a few days that Kirsten was a gifted all-around player. She's not the best hitter in the world, she's not the best passer, not the best blocker, not the best defensive player, but she is one of the best around at combining all of those talents.

So all of a sudden, we knew we had a right-side player, and a fine one. Now we started work on a second-tempo crossing-pattern offense, which we'd never been able to do. Illinois had never had that kind of a right-side hitter. Lisa Dillman came close, but she didn't have the consistency to pull it off. Kirsten did. In the second-tempo offense, we send a quick hitter into the middle to hit or to fake. Meanwhile, we keep crossing Kirsten left and right behind the first player, a very difficult play for the defense to stop. Kirsten is one of the best second-tempo hitters I have ever seen at the collegiate level, and that was a key to our offense, and another part of the surprise package Kirsten Gleis had become.

In early July, we hadn't known whether we had a team or not. We'd had an OK spring, but that's like spring football — so what, you looked good against your own second team; what does that say about how well you're going to do in the fall? The European trip gave us a lot of optimism, and Kirsten was better than we'd imagined. Now, as a staff, we had to make sure it all came together. We hammered them in practice. The first 20 minutes of practice were designed with such a heavy work load that no player could end the session and ask, "What do we do next?" Some of the Sports Performance club players had experienced this kind of training, and they knew what it meant. For the

Back Where We Belong 161

others, we wanted to shake them up and push them physically into unfamiliar territory.

When we got to Hawaii for the first tournament of the year and played UCLA, I knew we were going to be pretty good. We lost the match, but I could tell by the way that we passed and sided out with UCLA that we belonged on the floor with the best. Henderson and Gleis were passing well, Rogers looked good on the left side and Gleis on the right — this was going to be a good team.

The next night, we played Dave Shoji's Hawaii team, ranked fourth in the nation. When we beat Hawaii 3-0 in their gym, I knew that we were back to a Top 10-level team. Exactly how good we were going to be, time would tell.

This was the best I'd felt about coaching in two years. We'd gone 2-1 in a tough tournament, but the record didn't even matter. What mattered was that the players had played tough and aggressive against the best competition. We'd played UCLA hard down to the last point. We'd faced everything the home-town Hawaii crowd and team had to throw at us and outplayed them, something not too many teams do in Honolulu. And then against Houston, a match we needed to win and were supposed to win, we delivered. The players were beginning to conduct themselves in a championship fashion, on the court and off. We had some visitors on the trip, loyal fans from our "bowl-a-thon" auction, and our players treated our guests with courtesy and style. The 48-point plan and the 22-month program were paying off together.

The Illini Classic the next weekend was more of the same. There seemed to be one key moment after another in our season. The first was the UCLA match. The players and coaches both knew then, "Uh-oh, we're good — we're hanging in here, doing some things right." The second key moment was our comeback in Game 4 against Nebraska in the Illini Classic. Here we were, in an all-too-familiar situation the past couple of years. We led 2-0, then lost the third game badly. We were down 9-4 in Game 4 and Jay turned to me and said, "Is it going to be the same old thing?" At that point, there was nothing that any of us on the staff could do about it. I said, "We're just going to have to wait and see."

That's when Tina Rogers took over, drilling three con-secutive aces. Tina looked that adversity in the face and just stared the specter down, absolutely ripped three serves as hard as any I had ever seen, right down the line. That took guts, confidence and a fight-back attitude that had been missing for too long. We came back and won the game, and that might just have been the most telling moment of our season. It didn't hurt that it had come against our nemesis Nebraska, which was ranked ahead of us at the time — and stayed ahead of us even after we beat them. Then we beat Colorado for the championship, a match we should have won and needed to win.

Next up was Louisiana State in the Reebok Challenge in Chicago. This match figured to tell us a lot about our team. LSU and Illinois were very similar teams, both in the Top 20 in the preseason. Whoever won the match would probably catapult into a Top 10 position for the season, and the loser was going to linger down in the second 10. LSU had one advantage — they'd been to two consecutive Final Fours. On the other hand, we were facing them with a large, partisan crowd in suburban Chicago. We lost the first game 16-14, then won three straight pretty handily. By battling back from the first-game loss, we'd taken another key step.

We played Stanford for the Reebok title the next night. The Trinity Christian College gym normally seats about 1,500 fans. That night, the attendance was listed at 2,300. Fans were sitting everywhere, folding chairs set up three-deep all around the court. People were standing behind the court, behind the announcers, up on the balcony. You couldn't move and you couldn't breathe. And the crowd was as loud as it was big. There were lots of Illini fans — the Networkers had put together a fan bus — but there were people rooting for Stanford, too, because Marnie Triefenbach from Belleville was returning to her native state. The match was televised nationwide on SportsChannel.

We took the first two games and had lots of momentum, but Stanford came back to win. This wasn't like the two previous seasons, though — the coach let this one get away. I didn't demand that our offense go back to Tina Rogers late in the match. She was one of the reasons that we were ahead in the first place. Stanford had made some adjustments to stop Gleis, and I just wasn't alert enough to channel our offense back to Tina. She was getting frustrated because she wasn't getting the ball, and I don't blame anybody but me — I'm the one who's supposed to see that and correct it.

Back Where We Belong   163

Still, we had the chance to win the match. As I look at the tape, we only made one glaring mistake all night. Tina hit a ball into a block, a high block, and the ball fell down into the middle of our court with everyone watching it. It was just one silly error, the worst one we made in the match. We had a couple of serves that just ticked the tape for points against us in the rally scoring game, and we had one serve go long. It was an even match and could have gone either way.

Think about that: what if we had beaten Stanford that night? All of a sudden we're ranked No. 2 or 3 in the nation all year, Stanford doesn't get sent to the Mideast and we're in the Final Four with a good chance to win a national championship. Those little things in the rally scoring game — plus my failure to redirect the offense — came back to haunt us.

The next key moment was the following weekend, when we opened the Big Ten season at Ohio State and Penn State. At Ohio State, both teams were nervous and no one played very well. We won the match on athletic ability. The next night at Penn State was a real war.

Three things stand out from what would be our only Big Ten loss. First, Penn State played incredible defense early in the match, the best I've seen in 17 years of coaching. For about 45 minutes Penn State's defense was superb, world-class. That really got them excited and pushed us, threatened us. Second, we had an incredible run of bad luck with referees' calls. To this day, I look at the tape and can see that the referees were just dead wrong. Every call seemed to go against us. That's going to happen from time to time, both for and against us. Then, too, we were fatigued. We'd had a 4:30 a.m. wake-up call, a long trip, little rest. This figured to be the toughest road match of the season, and everyone was already exhausted going in. In the end, I have to congratulate Penn State. We had better athletes, but they refused to lose, beating us badly in Game 4 to tie the match and winning the rally scoring game 16-14.

After that we went on an incredible stretch of home matches with Iowa, Minnesota, Northwestern, Wisconsin, and Ball State — a three-week stretch when we played the best volleyball in my 10 years at Illinois. I don't know whether anyone could have beaten us. We were hitting around .400 as a team, Tina Rogers was unstoppable, and our defense, blocking and passing — everything was at a peak.

Outside of beating Penn State later in the season, my proudest moment was winning at Purdue in mid-October. We had left Lorna Henderson at home that weekend and were starting Julie Edwards in her place. Then after we beat Indiana on Friday night, Julie came down sick and we were down to playing Amy Brickley on the left side. We'd had so many gut-wrenching, painful losses at Purdue, it was a tough place to bring a wounded team. Purdue has the best record of any team in the Big Ten against Illinois. For us, it's not as big a rivalry as it used to be, but I think the Boilermakers still harbor some resentment over our supplanting them as the Big Ten's top team in the mid-1980s. This was our night, though, makeshift lineup and all: 15-8, 15-4, 15-12, a great win.

We were playing well, and most of the victories were fairly routine. In fact, somewhere along the line, we noticed we hadn't lost so much as a *game* since the Penn State match. Thirteen matches, 39 games without a blemish, and in five of those matches, we didn't give up 15 points *all night*. We were back where we belonged, dominating the Big Ten.

The way we were playing, the last thing we anticipated was a stiff test from Loyola. Don't get me wrong, it's not that I didn't expect Loyola to be good or to play well, but we were on such a roll. We had just won at Northwestern and Wisconsin, two tough places to play, two more three-game matches, neither opponent getting to 10 in any game. Then on a Sunday afternoon, we stopped at Loyola for a non-conference match.

Therese Boyle, the Loyola coach, had offered to play us in September before we flew to Hawaii in return for this match. She said, "Look, we'll be glad to do that; would you consider coming to play us at our place? It would do our program a lot of good to play a highly visible team in our home gym." Therese is a great person and had done us a favor by coming down for our opener, so we agreed to do it. There were times that afternoon I wished we hadn't been so accommodating. What a close call.

The Northwestern match had been Wednesday night, and we'd come home and gone up to Madison for a Saturday night match. On the way home Sunday, we stopped by for this afternoon match at Loyola. I knew our players would walk in there going, "What time is it? Let's see if we can get home early for dinner." And I knew this was going to be a really bad deal for us.

We won the first game easily and won the second game 15-0. I knew that that was dangerous. The team was on limited power to begin with, and I figured after the easy start they might just shut off the engines and start coasting. Sure enough, Loyola, nothing to lose, playing the behemoth from down south, came on like gangbusters. They won the third game, playing as well as anybody had played against us all year. They were just on fire — everything they touched went down, everything we hit was out of bounds.

Our 41-game winning streak was history, and the next thing we knew they were well on their way to winning the fourth game. I was committed to playing Megan Stettin in Game 4 to see what the freshman could do. We were down 14-8, but I was determined not to send the message that we couldn't beat Loyola with Megan in there. Jay Potter turned to me and said, "What are we going to do here?" and I said, "We're going to stick to our guns, we're going to do what we said we'd do."

I don't even remember who did it — the match is a blur to me, especially the fourth game — but somehow we came back. I think Kristin Henriksen and Merrill Mullis started to heat it up for us. Kristin basically said, "Enough — we're not going to lose this match." As soon as it ended, I went over to Therese Boyle and said, "You guys really deserved to win this match. If we were going to get picked off, it was today, and you guys really did the right things." No matter how good you are, you need a few breaks along the way, and we caught a break that day. Most of the season we had to make our own breaks.

A couple of weeks after that scare, we had a tough weekend in Michigan, probably our poorest efforts of the season. We lost a game at Ann Arbor and had to fight to win the match. Even Kirsten Gleis was subpar that night. Tina Rogers was off to her worst weekend of the year — and it would get much worse the next night. We didn't talk much about how poorly we were playing during timeouts or between games. We just stressed how important it was to compete. Michigan had beaten us up there the last two years, so obviously we had to respect them. It didn't matter if we were playing well or they were playing well, we just had to compete. If we get down, fight back. If we get ahead, you know Michigan will make a run, just try to fight 'em off. I was extremely relieved when we got through the match.

The next night, it was Michigan State — senior night for four MSU players, the last home match for head coach Ginger Mayson, and we were still playing poorly. Then early in the match, Tina Rogers went down with an ankle injury. The cards weren't on our side of the table, but we got through it. That was a case of a better team taking the night off, but still scoring the right points. It was also the last time we'd be able to get by on talent alone.

We'd won 16 straight Big Ten matches now, 48 of 49 games, but we still had some unfinished business to attend to — Penn State was coming to town, and since beating us in five games, they hadn't come close to losing a conference match.

Think about that: we hadn't won the Big Ten in three seasons, and this season we thought we could do it. But Penn State beat us, and they weren't going to lose unless we beat them. If we lost another match to anybody, we could forget about the conference title. One early loss on the road, just two points' difference in the rally scoring, had us walking the plank. All season long, there was the pirate with the sword, trying to poke us off the plank and dump us into the ocean. And there we were, every night, gathering our courage and our confidence, turning around and telling the pirate, "Sorry, but we're going to turn the tables on you. When this is all over, we're going to have the sword and you're going to be on the plank."

One misstep was all it would take. As you go through a conference season, every city, every arena is another nightmare waiting to happen. There are so many potholes to step in. But not only did our team avoid the potholes, it dominated, it lost only one single game. Remarkable.

I remember the locker room meeting after the Penn State loss. We knew we had dug a hole for ourselves; we knew we needed to win 18 Big Ten matches in a row. For me, it was a matter of keeping the team revved up through the season, in practice and in games. I needed to remind our players night after night that we needed to keep our guard up.

"This team is going to come after you," I'd tell them before every match. "This is going to be the biggest challenge of the season, not because their athletes are better than ours, but because *you're* going to have the temptation to take a night off. You're going be tempted to not work hard on a sequence of plays, and you're going to have to steel yourselves against those temptations. You're going to have to do it the right way, every play, all night. And you're going to have to do it 18 times."

After each win, the team would count down the victories they needed: "Right now — 17," then "Right now — 16." It seemed endless. We finally got it down to eight, seven, six, and they kept counting it down after every match. "Right now — five," and "Right now — four." And every time we would count one off, I'd look at the next match and remind the team, "Let's get ready right now for the next push."

That's what stands out more than anything else in 1992 — the march from the loss to Penn State in September through the Big Ten season to our victory over the Lady Lions in late November. Most people would say it was getting into the playoffs and coming so close to a Final Four berth, and those were highlights, no question. But it was that stretch of matches where we had no margin for error, where we had to perform, and we did — that's the crown jewel of the season to me.

I just kept harping away in every meeting. I kept it up until we got to Penn State, and then I backed off. It had been my job to help get the team past all the land mines leading to Penn State. Now I knew the hype and motivation would take care of itself. I didn't know the half of it.

That whole three-week period, from the time we finished the Michigan trip to the end of the playoffs, was like a whole different season for me. In a normal week, I'd go to the office, maybe get geared up for an interview, then return to the office and head to practice. A comfortable routine. In that three-week period starting in late November, it was late to bed, early to rise. The whole day, every day, was spent coping with the demands of a major sporting event. After the luncheon talks, interview sessions and press conferences, I'd watch miles of game films. Then on to a staff meeting, where we'd go over our strategy point by point, again and again. Now it's time for practice, an intense session that would leave players and staff drained. Then post-practice analysis, and more interviews in the evening. Everything not related to volleyball was like having to go out and get the newspaper or check the mail — something you had to get done, but nothing that was really going to rev you up.

In the middle of all this, I'd flip on the radio and hear someone talking about the ticket count for this week's match. I'd shake my head, marveling that this was as important to the fans as it was to us. All we're doing is playing a volleyball match. How is it that all these people can get so involved in this?

At this stage, for the first time I started to — not duck other commitments, exactly, but carve out as much space and time for myself as possible, so I could be in the right mindset for practice. I made a conscious effort to not lose a lot of energy over the other stuff.

I spend my life in a world of practice, game film and match preparation, and most people get only a glimpse of that side of volleyball. But on the other hand, I get only a glimpse of the public side of volleyball. Fans wonder what my side is like, and I wonder about the other side. I get snatches of what is going on, but I don't see it and experience it from start to finish. I marvel at the enthusiasm for Illinois volleyball, I'm proud of it, but I don't really experience it. It comes at me from all sides, from formal interviews to people on the street, and I have to be ready to talk about it, but that's not really my area of expertise.

Tina Rogers' ankle was one focus of the hype. We knew Tina wouldn't be able to play against Penn State. I've been around enough ankle sprains to know that it takes time for an injury that serious to heal. Even if she could somehow hobble out there, you have to be so mobile to play this sport, to spike and block. Lateral motion is crucial and she had injured her lateral stabilizing ligaments. Tina couldn't help us beat Penn State. Several times during the week before the Penn State match, I told the media that the chances of her playing were extremely slim.

Meanwhile, our trainer, Kathy Jobe, was getting involved in the hype, getting phone calls from the press and from our sports information department. She was suddenly experiencing what it was like to be visible and to say things that were going to be in print. She was learning about the pressure to guard against seeming uninformed. She and Mike Gernant, our team physician, had to do some homework because their evaluation of Tina's ankle was news. I was watching that with amusement. It was fun to see all these people involved, but we knew, Jay, Disa, and I, that Tina was not going to play. Tina may even have known. It was important that the issue be handled in an up-front manner, and as long as there was a mathematical chance that she could play, it had to be reported like that. It wouldn't have done any good for me to walk into a press conference and say, "Ah, there's no way." Tina's ankle had captured the interest of the community and the media covering our program, and I didn't want to deprive the community of that drama.

For an athlete like Tina, being in the center of that storm of attention must have been like being on another planet. A student-athlete is in class all day, then it's practice, the Varsity Room for dinner, and off to the library to study. Athletes often have such little spare time they don't even know what's in the newspaper or on radio or television. They don't know what is being said about them or how often anyone is talking or writing about them in the press, except in special, crazy circumstances like these.

Television crews, sportswriters, radio reporters and fans were at our practices all week — see Tina walk around the gym, see Tina soak her ankle in ice water, see Tina walk around the gym again. I was at home one night watching the news on television and there was a larger-than-life shot of Tina's ankle at practice. An ankle was drawing more television coverage than a lot of athletes get in an entire college career.

CHAPTER 15

CARDINAL RULES

Tina's ankle was a distraction that had a funny side to it. I couldn't see any humor at all in the controversy over Kirsten Gleis, a flap that was coming to a head at the worst possible time. Like many European athletes, like many European volleyball players at programs all over the nation, Kirsten chose to come to an American university for a year or two. It was our luck that she chose Illinois, and it was our misfortune — but thoroughly understandable, given her experience — that she chose to go home after just one year.

As far as I'm concerned, foreign players bring a different flavor to U.S. volleyball. They have a level of expertise beyond that of the average American college player, and they raise the level of play. We've played against great foreign athletes in other programs, and I've never had any objections. Whatever the rules are, whatever the structure is to bring foreign players into the game, go ahead and do that. Should there be a limit? I would say the sport has established its own limit already. I don't think there's an athletic director in the country who would allow a women's volleyball coach to stock his team with foreign athletes. I don't see it happening. So all this concern — Hebert has a Dutch player, Lisa Love at USC has a Peruvian, Mary Wise at Florida has a German, it's turning into a foreign game — I think that's more xenophobia than legitimate alarm.

And I can't think of any source for people's objections to our recruitment of Kirsten Gleis beyond that — she was a foreigner, and some people didn't want foreigners in our game. Almost exclusively behind my back, coaches within the conference, as well as from other parts of the country, were spreading the word that we'd committed violations in recruiting Kirsten. The word was being spread, and there was literally nothing to be done. At Illinois, our men's basketball team found out the hard way a few years ago that if somebody wants to take your program down, they can weave selected facts with irresponsible conjecture, and all your protestations of innocence, no matter how genuine, no matter how well supported by the evidence, won't save you from public condemnation or the wrath of the NCAA.

There was not one rumor about Kirsten that was true. Her recruitment was undertaken with meticulous attention to the rules. Do these people think I'm an idiot? Do they think Karol Kahrs is an idiot? This is a highly visible program, and anything we do can be called into question, and often is. We're going to go out and make a mistake, knowingly? With an Olympian, somebody people in this country have seen on television from Barcelona, someone widely known in volleyball circles? Karol would never allow anything to go uninspected in terms of a potential violation, and she was privy to every decision we made. Mark Williams in our admissions office spent months and months poring over Kirsten's transcripts. The Big Ten office was apprised of our recruiting effort early in the process. We formally asked the conference, "Would you please watch what we're doing? We'll send you copies of all the paperwork; let us know if we're out of line. We don't want to make any mistakes." The Big Ten monitored everything and gave us the green light.

We did literally everything we could to ensure that we acted above-board and in line with NCAA and Big Ten rules. And in spite of all that, these rumor-mongers, without talking to me or to Kirsten or to any of the principals involved, accused us of violating rules. And some of the rumors were ridiculous. Kirsten is one of the most honorable persons I have ever met, yet people were claiming that she had been paid to play volleyball in Europe — thus making her ineligible under NCAA rules. The rumor-mongers also speculated that Kirsten had no interest in academics, that she came to Illinois simply to play volleyball. If any of these people had bothered to check the record, they would have found Kirsten to be an excellent student, completing her year at Illinois with a near-perfect grade point average. But no one cared to check because it was easier to just spread rumors, particularly against a foreign athlete. And in the end, I believe that such anti-foreign feelings were at the root of the controversy surrounding Kirsten. What could be more professionally irresponsible? And then these people were telling recruits, "Don't go to Illinois — they'll just go out and recruit a foreign athlete."

Naturally, the rumors filtered down to parent groups at conference schools. At Wisconsin, an older man came out of the stands in a red Wisconsin Badger jacket and went on an obscene tirade toward me, Jay Potter and the program, labeling us cheaters. He never identified himself or made any pretense of engaging us in a real conversation, he just wanted to rant. He went up to Tina Rogers' parents and made the same accusations. A couple of weeks later, I was walking with Kirsten to do the radio interview after the match at Michigan when a man came out of the stands and stopped right in front of us, blocking our way. He pointed his finger at me, tapped me on the chest and said, "The NCAA's going to catch up with you bastards. You won't get away with this. You're cheating." Then he walked away. I found out later it was the parent of a Michigan player.

And the target of these rumors? Anyone who knows Kirsten Gleis knows this is a person who would never cheat or lie about anything. This is a person with as much integrity as anyone I've met in my life, not just in volleyball, but anywhere. A wonderful person, a great player and an excellent student. Despite having to overcome cultural and language barriers, she was a first-team All-American and graduated with honors. For such a quality person, a visitor to our country, to have to endure insults from these ugly Americans, it made me ashamed for my profession, ashamed for my sport, ashamed for my country.

And it was all started by a handful of people who thought they knew more about Kirsten Gleis than all our months of study had told us — and the Big Ten and the NCAA — about her. I've confronted some of those coaches, and basically what I hear from them is that they heard something from somebody else, and they repeated it, without having the guts to talk to me first. One time I actually told a coach all we'd done to comply with the rules, and he said, "Oh, I'm sure you have all the correct forms signed, but I know what really happened."

It's very difficult to ascertain how a foreign athlete can fit into our system. All the definitions are different — education, amateur standing — foreign athletes don't grow up with the same structures, so you have to interpret. This person played in this European competition — what does that mean for her American eligibility? But what you have to do, and what we did, is go to your campus interpretations officer, go to the conference, go to the NCAA, and get rulings.

Ultimately, I think the controversy erupted because Kirsten Gleis is one hell of a player, and she made a difference in where we finished, particularly on a team that had under-achieved for a couple of years. Even though we knew we were going to be good in 1992, the appearance of Kirsten Gleis surprised a lot of people. Who is this person, where did she come from? How the hell did Illinois get her? And because she was foreign, and there happens to be a crescendo of interest and concern now over foreign athletes, she had to suffer unjustly.

She was hurt very deeply by the accusations and the ill will, and that was one of the reasons she decided not to return in '93. The controversy took the edge off the season for me, as well. We were 32-4, we won the Big Ten title, we made it to the regional final, but I just couldn't enjoy the season the way I should have. Kirsten didn't deserve to be hounded like she was, and our program didn't deserve it, either.

We were helpless in the face of that distraction. The loss of Tina Rogers, devastating as it was, at least gave us a challenge we could come to grips with. As a coaching staff, we spent much of our time that week modifying our attack to take advantage of what Julie Edwards could do as Tina's replacement. A hitter like Tina Rogers erases a lot of errors. Your team can screw up on ball control, the passing and setting can be off, but Tina is so big and strong that she can rip the ball from anywhere on the floor and there is a good chance that the ball is going to go down on the opposite side of the net. In fact, at that point in the season, the odds were about 45 percent that any ball Tina hit was going to go down for a sideout or a point. We didn't have anyone else with a percentage even approaching that number in her position.

We were heading into the most important part of the schedule having to reinvent our offense, and I was preoccupied with that problem. When I face adversity, I immerse myself in evaluation of the problem and how to attack it. I may come across then as unsure of myself, but it really isn't like that at all inside. I get a little quieter, and my answers at press conferences may be less emphatic, but what I've done is to circle the wagons internally to hold off the next attack. Once I find the answer, I come out firing. During these periods of intense evaluation, people have told me I'm not being myself. But I've found I just don't have the skills to go into my intensive problem-solving mode and still maintain my usual confident style with the public and the press.

We planned to give Kirsten Gleis a wider range in her options with Tina out of the lineup, and all week long we practiced the things we expected of her. She did a great job and the team did an outstanding job of adapting to our changes. With Julie in the lineup in place of Tina, it improved our defense and ball control. We highlighted that part of Julie's game, as well as our serve-receive. We carefully analyzed how to use the personnel available to beat Penn State.

We hadn't blocked well in the earlier loss, so Jay Potter spent about 30 hours in front of the videotape machine planning just how we were going to block against Penn State. It was one of those matches where we felt we knew what Penn State was going to do before they did. We did a lot of double-teaming and anticipating the point of attack, switching our block. We had to practice that, it didn't just happen. You have to hone the recognition skills to pull it off. And once you have the information, you have to execute during the match. It's not like basketball where every time down the court you can set up in a zone or a man-to-man defense. In volleyball, there are six rotations and, in essence, six different games being played. The personnel in each rotation changes the game, and you have to play the game and coach the game in six different segments. Mentally, it is one of the toughest sports I have been involved with.

We had a good serving match as well. Defensively, we emphasized the placement of our back-row defenders as well as the placement of our block. We did a good job containing the Penn State offense — we took away the things they wanted to do and had them doing what we wanted them to do a great percentage of the time. I think they lost some confidence early in the match, and we just built on that.

In my 10 years at Illinois, it was one of our best team efforts in terms of studying a game plan and executing, even without one of our key players, to shut down a top team. I can't bring myself to say the word "perfection," no coach can, but we came about as close to a perfect match as we could.

People outside the program said, "Oh, Illinois played well tonight," but it was so much more than just playing well on one given night. It was the culmination of that two-month period of walking the plank, and it erased all the doubts that had dogged us since the loss. There's a fundamental feeling that comes just for a moment when it hits you that you have conquered, and it's worth everything. On the other side of the coin, it's just as tough when you've put everything on the line and you lose. But win or lose, the real memories are in the getting there, all the day-to-day things you go through to arrive at the moment where you have a chance to win.

It's hard to describe to people outside athletics what kind of experience that is, to build toward a special moment or series of moments during a season where you have to be at your absolute best. I don't think anyone can psychologically come up with that sort of keen focus every weekend. I can't describe the ingredients that go into that, but clearly, teams that are successful understand what it feels like to go through a series of prefatory events leading to that final moment of clarity and vision and peak performance that's required to win at an elite level.

A lot of things go into that — certainly practice — but so many parts of the life away from practice contribute, too: the media coverage, the slaps on the back by well-wishers. And then you get your own private moments, those few moments available to you right after you wake up, right before you fall asleep. And it's all visualization, planning in your mind what the big moment is going to look like, how it's going to feel. Everything contributes to the escalation of preparedness and intensity and anticipation of this great moment.

And when it finally arrives, at least for the good programs and for athletes who understand how to manage it and control it, it's a moment of absolute clarity. If you don't manage it correctly, it could turn into a sort of whirling dervish, chaos, and you won't be able to compete. But managed correctly, it puts you on a high plateau of keen awareness of what you're supposed to do. It can't be achieved often, maybe two or three times a season. But those who have been there understand it and know what it feels like.

After that victory, I was mildly concerned about the Ohio State match, but I banked on the fact that the community didn't realize how exclusively we'd been pointing toward Penn State. The fans were going to come out to see us clinch a share of the Big Ten championship and would be every bit as psyched up for this match as for Penn State. Our players might be thinking, "We

Cardinal Rules

don't have much left after the great high we were on against Penn State — we hope we win tonight," but the community's excitement would buoy the team. And that's what happened.

In the preparations before the match, the meetings, the meals, all the right words were said, but you could tell it just wasn't there like it had been the night before. This was the No. 3 team in the conference, after all; we weren't going to blow them out. I knew we'd need some breaks — some serves to fall on the end line, some calls from the officials — whatever breaks we could get. Sure enough, we played very sloppily but we played with confidence. The players knew they weren't going to play as well as the night before, but they never doubted they were going to win.

We gutted it out, a tough three-game match — we finished the season 59-4 in Big Ten games, a better record in games than in either of the seasons when we didn't lose a match — and we could hoist another banner. We were back where we belonged. Winning the Big Ten title — OK, OK, *sharing* the Big Ten title, though we felt like we won it, having beaten Penn State 3-0 after losing to them 2-3 — took a monkey off of my back. Athletics is a curious business. You can't rest on any success because the feedback on what you are doing is so immediate. If you win, you're a great coach. If you lose, you're a lousy coach.

Winning took a load off of the players' shoulders, too. All of these touted recruits had come to Illinois, drawn by our championships and tradition. The tough years had people wondering whether our program was a flash in the pan, whether our players' reputations were legitimate. Getting back on top in the conference answered that.

More than anything else, we'd earned the respect of the volleyball community again. "Illinois? Good team, good program." That in turn restored my confidence that I can build a winning team. It may take a little longer than I'd like sometimes, but I know I can get there. Now it was time to see how many more steps we could take.

We had to play Ohio State again six days later, winning 15-2, 15-7, 15-12, and then we beat Nebraska 3-0. The Ohio State match drew 4,271 to Huff Hall, a record that would last all of eight days, and the Nebraska match also drew more than 4,000. Beating the Cornhuskers was another key moment in our season. Nebraska is our archrival, more than any other team. Illinois and

Nebraska seem to have it in for each other in a healthy way, without any animosity. To beat Nebraska twice in one season — well, it's just not done. But now we were one step away from wrapping up the 22-month plan — returning to the Final Four.

In 1992, the NCAA had a modified regional seeding plan, for the most part leaving teams in the geographical regions. The exception is that if the two teams ranked in the top four are from the same conference, they'll be split, and I don't have any objection to what I call the "UCLA-Stanford rule." It would be awfully tough for a team that might be second-best in the country to have to sit out the Final Four because it also happens to be second-best in its own conference.

If I had a gripe in '92, it was that we didn't get the respect from the polls — and by extension the NCAA tournament committee — that I thought we deserved. We were obviously, by many accounts, better than Pacific, yet UOP was ranked No. 4 in the nation all year long. We beat Nebraska 3-1 and had wins over LSU and Hawaii, while Nebraska played a less-challenging schedule, yet they ranked the Cornhuskers above us because they've been good over the years and have also done a good job of lobbying.

Well before the pairings had been announced, I'd been hearing rumors about Stanford, ranked No. 2, being sent to the Mideast, away from top-ranked UCLA in the West. I felt strongly that the Mideast was the second-strongest of the four regions. That being the case, I thought Stanford should be sent to the South or to the Northwest. In the Final Four, you want the top seed, UCLA, playing the fourth seed, with the second and third seeds playing one another. I thought we should be seeded ahead of the South and Northwest. Every colleague I've discussed it with agrees, including Stanford coach Don Shaw. The NCAA selection committee apparently didn't see it that way.

The issue of regional seeding — keeping everyone close to home — versus national seeding — sending teams all over the country in an attempt to balance strength between the brackets — is probably the most divisive that has emerged in women's collegiate volleyball since I've been part of the game. On the one hand, several coaches on the West Coast, whose teams have historically been stronger than teams from any other region, want access to the Final Four. The rest of the country recognizes the merit of that argument, but our point is that we're not cultivating just one small plant, we're trying to cultivate an entire garden. A narrow focus on the West Coast lets that one plant flourish at the expense of the rest.

I've argued for a long time that regional seeding, letting each geographical region send a representative to the Final Four, leads to more growth in the different regions, as coaches and athletic directors see that they have a chance to have their programs move through the playoffs and arrive at the top level of competition.

People in men's basketball tell me that the NCAA tournament was seeded regionally until they got to the point where they had a national product, and then they went to national seeding. And they took that approach for the exact same reasons. When UCLA was dominating the tournament, there was a bottleneck in the West, and teams in other regions were getting into the Final Four that weren't as strong, but they did that to build the sport nationally, and there's no question it worked.

I've been disappointed in the shortsightedness of some of my colleagues in the West and the Northwest. They hurl the accusation frequently that people like me and Mick Haley at Texas and others with strong teams in the South and Mideast have selfish motives at heart, that we only want to give our teams a better chance to get to the Final Four. I resent that allegation — it's insulting to my intelligence and to my integrity — but more to the point it's so far from the truth it's ludicrous. How can someone look at my involvement in volleyball, from the early '60s to the present, all the things I've done to help the USA program and the AVCA, my work on national issues and not just personal Mike Hebert-Illinois issues — how can someone look at my record and then say I'd be so selfish, so myopic that I would push regional seeding just so my team could get to the Final Four? That's a childish kind of accusation, but it typifies some of the thinking.

You hear some West Coast coaches at the national tournament say things like, "This team from the South or the Mideast would finish fifth in our conference, and here it is playing for a possible national championship. That's embarrassing to the sport." Well, what's embarrassing to the sport is that kind of attitude. For one thing, you can't tell me Mideast and South teams haven't been competitive. I don't know of any embarrassing moment in the Final Four. The teams from the Mideast have competed very hard and very well.

But there are still people on the West Coast who feel they've been cheated, and that regional seeding makes a mockery of the search for the true national champion. I've never bought that, and I don't buy it now. My resolve on the issue is as strong now as it's ever been, probably stronger now that I've seen the impact nationally on the growth of volleyball in other areas of the country.

Now the national seeding committee, using the momentum of the expansion of the tournament from 32 teams to 48, has said, "Now that you've got a lot more teams in, we'll go to national seeding." I don't understand the logic of that, either. One of the facts that hasn't been addressed is that the number of Division I teams in each region is so imbalanced. The West and Northwest each have only 20 or so Division I volleyball schools, while the South and the Mideast each have around 100. But when it comes to making the rules for the sport, each region is represented equally on the NCAA Volleyball Committee. No wonder it's hard to build programs in the South. With 12 teams in a regional now, a West or Northwest team only needs to be in the upper half to make the tournament, and that's *with* regional seeding. And they want some slots in the South and Mideast, too? We feel just as strongly about getting redistricting relief from that imbalance as the West Coast people have felt about national seeding.

But I determined before the seedings were announced in '92 that if we did get stuck with Stanford, my response was going to be, "Great, bring 'em on. We almost beat 'em before." We couldn't ask for a better shot at beating Stanford than getting them at home in a regional final in front of our crowd. There was a part of me that really liked that scenario. And if we beat Stanford, nobody would be able to argue with our presence at the Final Four.

Stanford always seemed so focused, so alert, so confident last year — there was great chemistry on that team. As the match started, on the other hand, we were pretty ragged. Merrill Mullis was dishing the ball all over the place. Tina Rogers, who had played really well against Ohio State in the first round, her first match back after her injury, seemed distracted. She was playing a careful, safe game, no extra flair, no extra effort.

We got down 13-8, and it looked like it was going to be Stanford's night. I had inserted Kathleen Shannon at setter, and we started to come back. Kathleen's presence on the court was much more confident, and the team picked up on that. Kirsten Gleis, meanwhile, was excellent from start to finish — a big-time player coming up really big in the biggest match of the year. After the rough start, the rest of the team started playing well. Kristin Henriksen was sharp, Sue Nucci and Kellie Hebeisen were doing the job in the middle, all the role players were doing their part.

And suddenly we made a run. Hebeisen dished out a couple of aces, and when we tied Stanford at 13, it turned into one of the classic games in the program's history. That was when the Huff Hall crowd, earsplittingly loud all night long, hit its high note.

Fans watching me on the bench may have thought I didn't even notice the noise, that I looked almost relaxed. Inside, the computer banks were rolling at a high speed, and I couldn't let go of that or I might miss a move Stanford was making and fail to make the adjustment. Despite all the excitement and crowd, it's still a match with six players on each side of the net, and you each have a game plan and you try to execute that plan. But believe me, I knew the crowd was there, and I was glad it was on our side.

When the match gets to that point, the coach has a few moves to make, but to a great extent you just sit back and watch, knowing that both teams are playing well, and the winner is probably going to be the team that gets the bounce or the break or the call. Looking back, there were a couple of things that went against us. Kathleen Shannon was called for a lift on a spin move after turning around a quick set. It was really a touchy call at that point in the match. I'm not griping about it, those things happen. You just hope they don't happen at the wrong time in the match, and that was a really bad time for us.

Momentum in volleyball is critical, much more than other sports. The team serving keeps scoring points if it can put the ball away. It's so hard to change momentum, because the team receiving can do an amazing thing to put the ball over the net and on the floor and yet not score a point. To score, you have to do two amazing things in a row. A lot of people wondered why I took Kathleen out of that game after she had brought us back, and it was simply because we had to stop Stanford's momentum.

Volleyball is a rhythm game. Whistle. Serve. Receive. Boom. Whistle. Serve. Receive. Boom. All a coach has available to alter that rhythm are timeouts and substitutions. By stopping the flow of the match, sometimes you can disrupt the evolving confidence of the opponent. Late in Game 1, I had no timeouts and only one substitute left. I didn't want to put a back-row player in for one of the middle blockers because if the match lasted long enough, that player would be in a front-row spot. So the only logical move I had left was to put Merrill back in for Kathleen. I didn't want to change the chemistry because we had been playing well with Kathleen, but I had to try something to slow Stanford down.

Had we won the first game, I really believe we would have won the match, but we came up short, 17-15. As we exchanged benches, Don Shaw turned to me and said, "If every game's like this one, I'm not sure I can make it through this match."

The match hinged on that first game. We'd made a great comeback, but we couldn't get over the hump. Game 2, we'd spent ourselves emotionally in the comeback and we got down and couldn't ever mount a charge, losing 15-6. The third game was as good as the first, and just as a tough call had hurt us late in Game 1, we got the crucial call this time. Bev Oden hit a slide right at Merrill Mullis. Mullis dove on her back to avoid the ball. Don Shaw thought the ball grazed Merrill on the way out of bounds, and everybody was screaming "Touch!" or "No touch!" No touch was the call, and we won 17-15. I thought we were in the match again.

The difference in the fourth game, a 15-10 loss, was simply Stanford's execution. We played hard, they played hard, but Stanford didn't make quite as many errors as we did. They were just a little bit better than we were, and now they'd proved it twice, beating us in two very close matches. Our 22-month plan had worked to perfection, except for one little problem: we hadn't factored in Stanford.

Epilogue

  The gym's deserted now, footsteps raising an empty echo. We were tantalizingly close. But the loss to Stanford derailed our run at a national championship. No regrets from me, though. We played ourselves into a position to face Stanford in our own gym, winner goes to the Final Four. We had our shot, gave it everything we had, and came up a little short.

  Sure, I'd like to win an NCAA championship before I'm through, but if I don't, I won't feel like my career is diminished. We've won tournament championships, conference championships, and regional championships. I've felt what it's like to surprise people, I've felt what it's like to win as the front-runner, I've had wonderful receptions with my teams after winning championships. The only one I haven't felt is a national championship, and if I never get one, on the day I retire I'll probably say, "Gosh—I wish we could have done that one time, gotten a few breaks, or maybe gotten a little better coaching." That's about as long as I'll spend reflecting on it.

  But no matter what turns my life may take from here, Illinois volleyball will always be a source of great pride for me. It has been the centerpiece of my professional career. Things are in place now that will endure long after I'm gone. The championship banners will hang as permanent reminders of our success. A generation of young Illini volleyball fans will grow into adulthood remembering how much fun it is to watch Fighting Illini matches at Huff Hall. Thousands of people in our community have cultivated a genuine appreciation for female athletes and the exciting pace of volleyball. Most of these people now know the difference between a set and a spike, a middle blocker and a defensive specialist, a setter and an outside hitter. The local media corps — our hard-working radio, television, and newspaper folks — have learned the game and have become nationally acclaimed as architects of state-of-the-art coverage of volleyball. And recently, Illinois has become the nation's leader in event attendance. Virtually none of these things were in place when I arrived in 1983. It is humbling to think I've had such an impact.

Yes, we lost to Stanford, but there's no point looking back, unless you can learn something from it. I've lived several lives, and I think I've learned something from each of them. The fatherless kid stumbled his way through college, a stint in the Peace Corps, political activism, marriage, fatherhood, teaching, and coaching. To this day, I believe in all of the truths I stood up for in my youth. I don't regret a single stand I took.

There are still days when I think I should be applying my talents to the continuing struggle against racism, to the effort of helping MIA families resolve their anguish and move forward, or to the search for economic justice on a world scale — something socially significant. But as I've grown older, I've realized that if you can find an environment in which you can function successfully, and if you can get up every day and find something to like about what you're doing, you'd better hold onto that pretty tightly. If at the same time you can have a positive impact on the people in your immediate environment, that is as much as anyone can ever expect.

I know I've had players come into my program who are racially insensitive, because of the environments they've come from. I'd like to think that, without my ever having to confront them directly, just being around me for four years, their behavior will be different. I feel the same way about players who show up with poor time management skills, poor communication skills, or with a naive perspective on how to grow into a responsible adult. I think I can be a role model and make a difference in how they prepare to enter the outside world.

The people who spend most of their lives solving international problems and winning Pulitzer Prizes are very special, and I have all the admiration in the world for them. As for me, I just want to make a difference. And recently, I've been making a difference by coaching volleyball players. But whether I'm a coach, a father, a teacher, a husband, or whatever else lies ahead of me, I *always* want to make a difference.

The fire still burns.

Check out these other exciting sports titles from Sagamore Publishing.

To order with check or money order:
Send order (book cost plus $3.50 shipping for 1st book; $.50 for each additional book) to:

> Sagamore Publishing
> P.O. Box 647
> Champaign IL 61824-0647

To order with VISA/MC call (800) 327-5557

_____*Against the World: A Behind-the-Scenes Look at the Portland Trail Blazers' Chase for the NBA Championship*
ISBN 0-915611-67-8 $19.95

_____*Best in the Game: The Turbulent Story of the Pittsburgh Penguins' Rise to Stanley Cup Champions*
ISBN 0-915611-66-x $19.95

_____*Bitter Roses: An Inside Look at the Washington Huskies' Turbulent Year*
ISBN 0-915611-80-5 $19.95

_____*Blue Fire: A Season Inside the St. Louis Blues*
ISBN 0-915611-55-4 $22.95

_____*Charlotte Hornets: Sharpening the Stinger*
ISBN 0-915611-82-1 $19.95

_____*Dawn of a New Steel Age: Bill Cowher's Steelers Forge into the '90s*
ISBN 0-915611-81-3 $19.95

_____*Down for the Count: The Shocking Truth Behind the Mike Tyson Rape Trial*
ISBN 0-915611-78-3 $19.95

_____*The Fighting Irish Football Encyclopedia*
ISBN 0-915611-54-6 $44.95

_____*Glory Jays: Canada's World Series Champions*
ISBN 0-915611-68-6 $19.95

_____*Hail to the Orange and Blue*
ISBN 0-915611-31-7 $29.95

_____*Lady in the Locker Room: Uncovering the Oakland Athletics*
ISBN 0-915611-70-8 $19.95

_____*Lou Boudreau: Covering All The Bases*
ISBN 0-915611-72-4 $19.95

_____*Marge Schott: Unleashed*
ISBN 0-915611-73-2 $19.95

_____*New York Rangers: Broadway Blues*
ISBN 0-915611-85-6 $19.40

_____*Phil Rizzuto: A Yankee Tradition*
ISBN 0-915611-71-6 $19.95

_____*Phoenix Suns: Rising to the Top With the "Team of Oddities"*
ISBN 0-915611-84-8 $19.95

_____*Pittsburgh Pirates: Still Walking Tall*
ISBN 0-915611-69-4 $19.95

_____*Roll Tide Roll: Alabama's National Championship Season*
ISBN 0-915611-79-1 $19.95

_____*Stormin' Back: Missouri Coach Norm Stewart's Battles On and Off the Court*
ISBN 0-915611-47-3 $19.95

_____*Take Charge! A "How-To" Approach for Solving Everyday Problems*
ISBN 0-915611-46-5 $9.95

_____*Undue Process: The NCAA's Injustice for All*
ISBN 0-915611-34-1 $19.95

_____*Winning Styles for Winning Coaches: Creating the Environment for Victory*
ISBN 0-915611-49-x $12.95

_____*Woody Hayes: A Reflection*
ISBN 0-915611-42-2 $19.95